# Contents

# INTRO

First, all my thanks to my parents, without whose support and patience, this book would never have come about. Never. Massive thanks too, to everyone that came to Las Vegas with me over the years, everyone that I met there and showed me what's what, and anyone else that has been cornered by me over the years, to have to listen to me go on, and on, and on about Vegas, all the while without becoming violent towards me (this is an achievement of high renown, I can tell you). To the rest of you...I hope that some of my Vegas can be of help to you or yours and many thanks for picking this up!

Right so! I'm thinking that you've either bought or been given this book as you're someone that really appreciates the bright side of life whenever you can. I like the bright lights too, of course, or this would never have seen the light of day. First of all, the negative...this book isn't entirely comprehensive (with Las Vegas, this is almost an impossibility), in my opinion, but saying that, it's got much more than you'll need to have a most fantastic Las Vegas experience over and over again, along with saving you money.

Hi! (Only two paragraphs later... dreadful manners, apologies). My name is Shane, Shaner to lots. There have been other names too. Shan-o, Don-no,

Donaldson, Rosario, Hamish, The Dublin Bun. Yeah, I'm not sure why either but hey-ho. All coolio. You can call me anything you like, I'm well used to that by now. I'm a "mentally stable with quirks" (so I'm assured) Dubliner, from Ireland, who has been very fortunate, in that I got to travel for holidays/vacations numerous times, and also got to live on occasion, for a few months at a time, in Las Vegas (with the 90 day ESTA visa). To be honest, barely an hour passes when I don't think about friends living and working there, the place itself of course, and the great times that I've spent there.

My friends there, I'm so lucky to have met some truly wonderful and unique people. People that you'd never forget. They told me so many of the locals' secrets firsthand, and really, if you want to get to know the place, that's the best way to enjoy Las Vegas, with the locals. They really do know what we don't. There's no doubt. It was a couple of trips in for me before I really met some of them, and luckily for me, became friends. The people of Las Vegas are some of the nicest people that I've been fortunate enough to get to know in life. Too difficult not to like!

Listen (we often start sentences in Ireland with "listen" so ignore that. It's mainly for emphasis), let me explain further. I'm not rich, and I don't have a huge desire to be. This makes no odds to you I'm sure, and that's coolio, but what will help you by me not being rich, is that when I go to Las Vegas, whether it's for a holiday or for a nicer stay of a few months of a holiday, I do it in such a way as to get the best that I can get for the best price that I can get. Don't ever let anyone put you off going on a trip to Las Vegas by hearing them say "ah yeah, Las Vegas eh? it's way too expensive". That's not really a fully balanced statement. Yes, it's become more expensive over all, undoubtedly, and I absolutely HATE those resort fees, but there are still many many ways to really have the Las Vegas experience at a lower price by being clever with things. In this book, I'm going to show you how so no worries. There are also lots of inexpensive places to eat and drink, places to stay, etc. Take this from me, I DO NOT have major money, Las Vegas can really be done on nearly any budget, there really is something for everyone, and I do know where many of the great deals are.

My "real job" (I'm self-employed) is finding e-commerce sellers, who sign up to my service, products to sell very profitably on Amazon in the U.S, so I know exactly how to find you whatever you'll need in Las Vegas at a very good price PLUS, you can visit my site sometime if you fancy it. Functionally, it contains more, and there are offers for you there that aren't in this book. The site is, and I didn't pick the name, let me be clear on that... my sister-in-law is responsible, anyway, it's at www.shanelovesvegas.com. On that, shanelovesvegas.com, throughout this book, you might see the term "DOS" pop-up in various areas. This means that I have a deal on the site for this. DOS - Deal on Site. That's all.

In Las Vegas over the years, I've stayed in all types of hotels, from the most luxurious 5 stars to 3 stars, getting great deals on ALL, or I CAN DEFINITELY ASSURE YOU…I wouldn't have been staying there! Likewise, with bars, restaurants, shows etc. This book is going to help you with all of this. A total pleasure for me, as this is one of my passions, finding deals for people (a significant component of my "real job"). Nice to combine it with Las Vegas, a very, very, serious passion! I really get a buzz from seeing people smiling and happy from something that I might have helped them with. So, by you having this book in your hand you've already helped me to get my buzz

All my best for now, and I really hope that you enjoy this book, just as much as the experiences I've had so that this could come about.

Shane(r).

Enjoy!

# CHAPTER 1 - SOME FREQUENTLY, AND SOME RARELY ASKED, QUESTIONS ABOUT LAS VEGAS

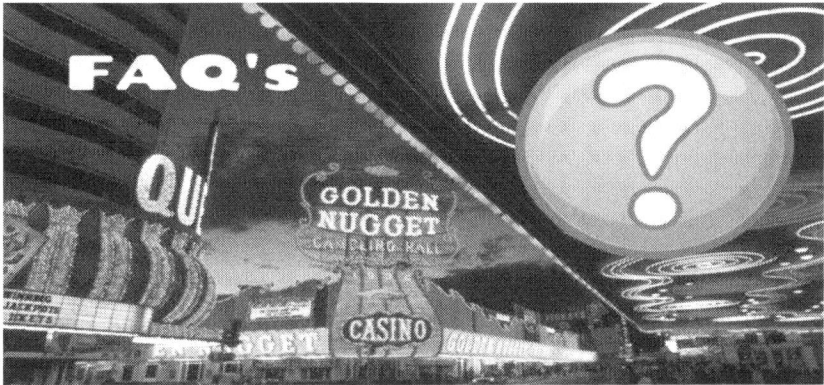

## Can I booze away in public?

Like on the Strip and outdoors? Yep (!), but use a to-go cup and read on. You're not allowed to carry glass containers on the Strip. You can't drink on the CAT (Citizens Area Transport) buses, nor can you eat or smoke on them. Also, no alcohol drinkin' on the Monorail. You can't drink within 1,000 feet of a church, synagogue, public or private school, hospital, substance-withdrawal-management facility, and homeless shelter. You CAN walk right into a casino with your drink but you CAN'T take your "outside" drink into bars or clubs. That's that explained hopefully!

## I've another booze question. What age do I have to be?

We've only just started and already two booze questions! I like this! You have to be 21 and most likely you're going to be asked for I.D. even if you're 71.

## And gambling/gaming? What age for that?

21 too.

## Back to booze! Is it true that I could really buy drink 24 hours around the clock in Las Vegas?

Haha! Yep! If you want to. You really love the sauce, don't you? Hard to blame you, but it's going to cost you a bit unless you're clever about it. You should look at the Happy Hours and Reverse Happy Hours for sure (you can find them in the guide at the end of the book) and also, if you're partying hard, get some drinks for walking around with, and for your room, definitely for your room, from the supermarkets (there are plenty of them off the Strip) or Lee's Discount Liquor is a good spot. I'd definitely be doing that if I were you. If you don't fancy going to the supermarkets but could do with booze and/or food, cigarettes or what have you, being brought to you, use Pikfly.com (not cheap but they do booze), Instacart.com (food and booze), Grubhub.com (food), Postmates.com (food and pills for your headache, stomach etc.), and Ubereats.com (food). This will be invaluable when you have your crash day or just fancy a rest. Because clearly, you'll need a day to get yourself back into some sort of proper state as you've already asked me three drinking questions and I have lots of experience of feeling like this!

### The Las Vegas Tunnel People. Are there really people living in the tunnels? Can I go in there?

Ok, hold your horses for a second before you go scooting down into the tunnels singing Mary Poppins numbers. There are 200 miles of Storm Drains running under the Strip and in the Valley. I lived beside one of them on a couple of occasions and very often saw the "Tunnel People" (as the TV show called them, I'm not making up this term) coming and going. They slept in behind the bushes as well, outside the apartment block from what I could tell. The bushes were only a few feet away from the entrance that they used to the tunnels which was a ripped down fence. They never approached me so I left them be. I often wanted to give them something but apparently, it's against the law. That's a tough law. I don't like it. Why should a person be prevented from giving what could be considered to be a less fortunate man or woman, a gift of some sort? It's not allowed though, and that's very sad. Many of these folks live in the tunnels because of mental illness, etc., and I would advise NOT going into them. There are estimated to be 1,000 people living there. Would you fancy being woken up by total strangers popping into your home uninvited? No, probably not. Especially if you're not in the best of form. Live and let live.

**Earthquakes! What's the craic? (Pronounced "crack" in Ireland, meaning, "what's the story?" and not the drug. Totally lost in translation at times from Irish English to English. Maybe don't use this word too much unless you get a chance to explain what it means as you'll have a very confused and concerned audience).**

The "craic" is actually the San Andreas Fault. Nevada is in third place of the states for the frequency of earthquakes. Seismologists state that there's roughly a 1 in 10 chance that an earthquake (of magnitude 6), one large enough to cause significant damage, will strike the valley in the next 50 years. It's believed that the San Andreas Fault, if it produced an earthquake of 8 or more on the Richter scale could cause absolute chaos in Las Vegas, even with it being hundreds of miles away, and then there was one just yesterday in the Californian Desert, felt Downtown. Plus, one July 5th this year, also California.

## Can I take a photo in the Casino?

Good that you asked! Very nice manners! Hmmm. Hmmm. Hmmm. This is a tricky one. I've been stopped in the Wynn and Cosmopolitan taking pics before. In the Wynn, actually, nope, it was both in the Wynn and in Encore (Wynn's sister hotel). In the latter, I was trying to get one of a Willy Wonka Machine. A quick one here. People go to Las Vegas, some to disappear, others for other reasons, and some just don't want to be pictured gambling on Willy Wonka machines, and/or drinking, and/or smoking. In the Cosmopolitan, when I was stopped, it was explained to me, and the guy was totally cool with me taking pics of the Sharknado machine (that was for you Joe if you're reading), ONCE there were no people that weren't with me in it. Just be discrete, take your selfies, pics of your pals eating or drinking, posing with whatever it might be, but don't take them of anyone gambling. Also, you can't use your phone in the Sportsbooks.

## If I'm not staying in a Casino, can I still visit it?

Definitely, they'll be delighted to have you!

## What's the least expensive time to visit Las Vegas Shane?

December, the couple of weeks before Christmas. I've been there most Decembers over the last eleven years or so, more often than not. Great deals at this time including flights. July and August can be good too but very very hot. After Christmas Eve though, prepare to pay through the nose with New Year's Eve being the busiest night in Las Vegas.

## And what would be the worst time to go financially speaking?

On New Year's Eve. It's incredibly crowded. If you don't like crowds, I wouldn't even think about it if I were you. Likewise, Labor Day, Memorial Day and Independence Day. The Super Bowl can be very busy and when CES (Consumer Electronics Show – I can't wait to go to this regardless) is in town, there can be big crowds. It can also be expensive when the Electric Daisy Carnival (June) and Life Is Beautiful (this has been on in April and October, on different years) events are on.

## Prostitution. Is it legal in Las Vegas? I'm asking on behalf of this dude that I met in the pub a while ago. He asked me to ask you as his uncle's friend's cousin's uncle's friend wants to know.

No. You can tell that dude in the pub that you "met a while ago," to tell his uncle, to tell his friend, to tell their cousin, to tell their uncle, to tell his friend, that they'd have to venture outside Las Vegas. Phew! It's like the end of that Crocodile Dundee film this, down in that subway station. That shouldn't have been so difficult. Anyway, there are legal places further afield. Google will find them. Google finds everything.

**Water, man! I'll be in the Desert, WOW! I'm actually bloody going!!! WOOHOO! What about water man?**

You sound excited, YES! Super! Stay that way! Water... Drink it, drink lots of it. Otherwise, you might just collapse. I did one day from dehydration, anyway, that's for another day. Again, drink lots of water. You're in the Desert remember? For every alcoholic drink, have a pint of water. Obviously, I didn't heed this myself many times, but I wish that I had done. The booze can trick a person, and that's part of how it works of course. Tap Water in Las Vegas, no, don't drink too much of it. If you're only here for a few days, it'll probably be fine. I'm not a doctor though so it's your call. Plenty of people with kidney stones in the city (high levels of magnesium and calcium). You can go to the local supermarkets and refill a gallon or so for less than 50c.

**Shane, I'm almost broke and need to keep some money but still, I want to buy booze and still enjoy my last few days in Las Vegas. How can I pay supermarket prices?**

You're cool! Do just that! You're really answering your own question. There are plenty of Supermarkets. You're a man/woman after my own heart as we say in Ireland. It means, we're similar in this respect. There are Smith's, Walmart's and Albertsons in large numbers close to most parts of the Strip. Just use your Uber or Lyft app and they'll have you there in no time at all. I used to get ENORMOUS (1.75 litres from memory, which is tricky with this drink) bottles of Fireball for $18 or so at Albertsons. Happy Daze indeed! Also, my guide at the end of this book, give it a look and you'll drink very well and for great value, if you do it right, and you'll be in a bar/pub. :)

**I miss home a bit. I want to buy food from my own country. Are there any options? I really shouldn't have left home, should I?**

Haha! You're cool! It's all good. Las Vegas has you covered. Go to the International Marketplace at 5000 S. Decatur Ave. near W. Tropicana. There's also "99 Ranch Market" the Asian-specialty supermarket chain in Chinatown (Las Vegas has a Chinatown!) and it's at W. Spring Mountain and Wynn Road. Oh, and for the

Irish among you, Walmart sells Kerrygold butter. I think it's about a fiver for half a pound, expensive yeah, but it's Kerrygold in the Desert yo! Make sure you can get it to the fridge quickly or things will get very melty very quickly and you could go on fire from the sun. You won't go on fire from the sun... at least not under these circumstances, hopefully.

**I might take a trip elsewhere too. What about Reno, Los Angeles and San Francisco, are they far away from Las Vegas?**

Not really that far. Reno is 439 miles, LA is 270 miles and San Francisco is 569 miles, so you could be in any of them in an hour on a plane, well, maybe San Francisco can be just slightly over an hour at times.

**How many people live in Las Vegas? Lucky ducks!**

On the 2016 figures, 623,747 but that's just for the city. The Las Vegas metropolitan area has a population of over 2 million.

**They get lots of tourists in Las Vegas, don't they?**

Yeah, they do! They had 39.01 million of us in 2018. Nice numbers those ☺

## How much does an average hotel room cost in Las Vegas per night?

That's a brilliant question! It's a tiny bit complicated however, and this is averaged across hotels of far different standards as regards quality and service. The Las Vegas Review-Journal has figures on this. Across the board, the figure in January 2017 was $150.21 as the average cost per room per night, stay with me here, there's more. This does NOT include resort fees, parking or taxes. When this is broken down further (again the resort fees, parking or taxes are not included), the average daily rate for the Strip hotels is $163.72 and for Downtown (Fremont), it's far lower at $74.59. Not the ideal time to do this analysis as January has CES (Consumer Electronics Show) and New Year's Day falls into the calculation but this gives you more of an idea. I'll be helping you to try to dodge these prices obviously, as I'm really not keen on paying those higher amounts when they can be avoided with a bit of planning and looking around.

## Ok, what about the heat, is it really hot?

June to August is very hot. June to August average a high of 39.33 C, which is just shy of 103 F. It can get higher as this is the average high for these months. Over the entire year, the average monthly is 27.5 degrees Celsius, which is 81.5 F. In winter, around

Lyft and Uber Apps, I'll explain more further on. They will help you get around IF you haven't used them before. I have codes that will save you moolah off your journey, (you can get them on my site, shanelovesvegas.com) and will save you quite a bit overall if you're moving around. Madness to use taxis instead, sheer madness. Just DO NOT use taxis if you're in the money-saving game.

**I haven't a rashers (a clue) about gambling, and I'm off to Las Vegas very soon. How can I sort this? Should I cancel the trip? I think I might be having a panic attack.**

You're not having a panic attack, you're totally cool! In fact, you sound "sort of" like me on my first trip to Las Vegas, so believe me, these are normal feelings and you are A1A Beachfront Avenue OK! Because I was (as soon as I landed). If you're really not, please talk to your Doc, or a Doc, as again, as per other places on this site, unfortunately, I'm not medically qualified to help you, but from here, you're fine/grand/all good. First things first, you do not have to gamble. Also, I'm not really a gambler (I will the odd time, Blackjack, Roulette, Keno, there's a game at the Wynn that I like too, it may be called Red 8? They have a great Asian restaurant there by that name so I think that's what this game is called too, lovely food, not exactly cheap though, yet affordable luxury certainly) but I do know that there are many casinos that offer free lessons. You'll be cool! Here you go, save you looking them up as I can tell you're a bit stressed out, but again, you're fine! Boulder Station, Circus Circus, Excalibur, Gold Coast, Golden Nugget, Luxor, Palms, Planet Hollywood Resort & Casino, Rampart Casino at The Resort at Summerlin, Strat (formerly The Stratosphere) and Tropicana.

## Is Las Vegas Safe?

Well I've had my jaw broken in two by a lunatic (with a huge bill after being in three hospitals and surgery. MAKE SURE THAT YOU HAVE HEALTH INSURANCE AND TRAVEL INSURANCE), so I'd probably be a prime candidate to tell you that it's not safe, but in the main it is. As with everywhere, you need to keep your eyes open. If you stay on the Strip or Fremont (Downtown) you should be fine. Don't do the side streets especially when it's dark, they can be sketchy for sure. Stay alert in the car parks. Don't buy water or those VIP passes off the street vendors on the Strip, and those last two points aren't entirely relevant to what you asked, but it's good for you to know. The water bottles have been refilled from taps is what I'm being told. On the Strip, I've been offered new iPhones and high-end laptops amongst other things. Just don't do it. You know why yourself. Karma and goodwill to others. Be aware of pickpockets too. The pickpockets will watch you at the

ATM (cash machines) and in Souvenir Stores to watch where you keep your wallet/purse. Then they will try to bump you (and then pickpocket you or have an accomplice do it) or sell you something by waving it in your face. That three-card monte game you see being played on the Strip too, avoid that.

**What's going on with these resort fees? What are they, and do I "have" to pay them?**

Filthy, filthy dirty words these. When I first started going to Las Vegas, this wasn't a thing at all. I don't like the practice, not at all, but it's here in full-flow and it's pretty much unavoidable, except in certain resorts IF you take a very expensive upgrade and that's not always the case either. If you're booking a room and the resort fee isn't mentioned, the likelihood is that the first you're going to know of it is when you get hit with it as you check out of the hotel. Bit shitty eh? Bad enough being hit with it, but on the last day? Naw. There are very few Las Vegas hotels without the resort fee and the charge is from (these figures are WITHOUT tax and PER day) $8.95 (El Cortez, it's Downtown) to $45 (Venetian and Palazzo). So, in practice, if you're staying five nights at The Venetian or The Palazzo, you'll be paying $225 in resort fees plus tax when you checkout. Both incredibly beautiful resorts it must be said, albeit at the higher $45 side on the resort fee.

The resort fee generally covers:

Free internet access, a Daily Newspaper, Free boarding pass printing and free local phone calls. Sometimes gym or spa access. To note, and for fairness, both The Venetian and The Palazzo (sister hotels) offer two guests access to Canyon Ranch SpaClub (it's really top notch!) as part of the resort fee, the other bonuses just mentioned, and one two-for-one drink coupon for well drinks, domestic beer, or wine at any casino bar excluding the pool decks. So, this resort fee isn't all bad BUT I'd prefer the choice if it was down to me as I'm really not cool with paying $45 plus tax extra per night unless I'm getting a super deal. I'm not going to pay it if I can avoid it. It's not a practice I can align with.

now...THIS IS COOL! LISTEN UP TO THIS... If you play the Wynn Slots App, you can get up to four free nights in the Wynn (an outstanding hotel-casino resort), and if you're travelling with someone, have them do the same and suddenly you have eight nights, and currently, they are NOT charging RESORT FEES on these offers. You can find this on my site, shanelovesvegas.com, in the "Apps" section.

## What's the best way to get to my hotel from the airport?

The long and the short of it is use Uber and Lyft. If you haven't downloaded these apps previously, only do it when you get to America (if you're coming from abroad) and as I previously mentioned, I have some codes for you to use that will save you some Dolla Dolla Billz. These are on the site. Alternatively, if your hotel offers a shuttle, you could get that. Do NOT get a taxi. That's simple enough. IF you do decide, "screw this Shane, I've had a long flight, I just want to get to my hotel" and get a taxi, DO NOT let them take the tunnel. Use Google Maps and know the roads that you want to take. If you tell them (the taxi drivers) the route, by law they must take it. There are some free shuttles but not really to the major hotels, although Harrah's and The Orleans have them. There are other shuttles from Bell Trans. They fit 24 passengers. This is a Share-A-Ride service and you will be sharing the vehicle with up to twenty-four other travelers and may stop between 3 to 5 hotels before reaching your destination. Direct transportation to your hotel or airport is NOT guaranteed. The cost is $15 to $18 for a round trip. Maybe not the best bet for you, nor for me. I'd prefer to use Uber or Lyft, but just giving you your options of course.

**I'd like to bring my pet to Las Vegas. Is there anywhere that we can stay together?**

Cool, that's nice! I won't bring Dolly Donuts (my little lady), the flight would be too difficult from Ireland for her. So, here's what I know as regards pet-friendly hotels. I'm going to give you some of the bigger ones here. Trump, Cosmopolitan, Four Seasons, Vdara, Delano, Linq, Flamingo, Mirage and lots of the less famous ones. You ought to check first though as I'm not an expert on this matter having never brought a pet overseas. IF you're bringing your doggie in the hot weather of the summer, buy them some dog shoes, as the sidewalk will burn their paws and no one should put their pet through that. Funny the things that we might not think of, eh? I hadn't even considered this being from a colder country but this is definitely a thing you should be doing.

**I'm very keen to go shopping. What are my options?**

Well, where do I start with that? There are so, so many places. Las Vegas is a shopping Mecca. I'll do a piece on this again but just to give you something quickly right now. If I was shopping the places that I'd go to would be Las Vegas North Premium Outlets (the CAT bus will get you here for the least cost), Fashion Show Mall (opposite the Wynn) and the Forum Shoppes at

Caesar's Palace, the Miracle Mile at Planet Hollywood and The Grand Canal Shoppes at the Venetian. There are many more but that's for another day. You should sign up to the Premium Outlets site BEFORE going there and you'll get so many coupons off what are already great prices. IF you haven't data on your phone (I'm thinking of those who are travelling into America with a foreign mobile provider), the Wi-Fi can be patchy at the North Premium Outlets so in this case print your coupons at home or they might let you do it at the hotel if you ask nicely, I'd do it at home though to make sure I'd done it, and anyway, who wants to trawl around a hotel looking for a printer? This is good holiday/vacation time!

**I'm quite wary after hearing stories of huge ATM fees for withdrawing money in the Casinos.**

That's cool and you're dead right to be. Bit of advice for you here. First, unless you absolutely must, do NOT use the ATMs etc. in the hotels and casinos as they tack on some serious charges. Some of the machines have $6 charges and that's just the immediately visible stuff. If you need to withdraw money, I'd go to one of the banks to do this. Also, when you're shopping etc., some ATMs or POS (point of sale) terminals (they are the machines that the staff in the shop get you to insert your card in, or tap your card on), they might ask you whether you would like to complete the transaction 'with conversion' or 'without conversion', you should ALWAYS choose 'without conversion'. There's no further debate on that one unless you like handing away money. Also, you could use a Revolut card. More on the site on that one.

**I have an absolute belter of a hangover, and/or I just fancy doing nothing for the day and recovering in my room. I really don't want to leave it, BUT I'm in no state to deal with the public, and I really don't want to pay room service prices for food, and I just might need a little drinky to sort my head out, and then maybe I'll get it together and go out later. I can't write this question any further. I'm in pain Shane. That actually rhymes, doesn't it (?) or is it my head (?) and I understand that I'm making demands here. Please help me!**

Hahahahahaha! This is very like me with a hangover! I have you sorted on many levels if you can read this with your headache that is. You don't believe me? Ok, this is what you do. For pain relief for your headache or stomach use Postmates (www.postmates.com) as they'll get you non-prescription medication if you need it. Also, you can use Postmates to order from all sorts of food outlets and stores from them. Smoothies, breakfast, lunch, and dinner. Denny's, Subway, Carl's Jr, Fatburger, White Castle, McDonald's, 7Eleven Convenience Stores, and really, that's just the tip of the iceberg. I have this App listed for you on my site also.

Booze? You want booze too? Is that what you're telling me? Didn't you have enough last night already? Just messing with your hangover. Haha, I know, it's ok, coolio, you're in Vegas, of course, you're right! Ok, just wait for a second though. I want to make sure that you're getting fed first. You could use Pikfly.com or Instacart.com for your booze. These are on the site too.

Back to food, if you haven't found what you need on Postmates, you could use UberEats, GrubHub, or DoorDash, all on the site.

## Should I tip in Las Vegas? If so, how much would be considered appropriate?

Yes, Las Vegas runs on tips. A quick rule – DON'T tip with chips (it's actually breaking the law, gambling chips that is, not potato chips. I don't know the legality of tipping with potato chips). Similarly, with the cash out tickets from the machines, some casinos are ok with their staff receiving them, but in general, don't. You could be putting them in a position where they might be suspected of taking it from a machine. Use cash, it's much more straight-forward and no one ends up in front of a judge.

Housekeeper – $2 and up per night is good. Leave a note to say thanks for cleaning the room or they won't take it. The staff working on Sunday's get the most tips as that's when most folks check out, so try to do it every day instead, as the staff during the week might not be working on Sunday. If they bring something to you, tip them for this too, $2 minimum is good.

Casino Host – some aren't allowed to take tips or gifts. If they are, put it in a thank you envelope, it can be an e-gift card or something similar. Maybe something for their partner or their kids. This is acceptable, once they are allowed.

Limo Driver – $20

Curbside Porter – these are independent contractors (not airline employees). You don't have to avail of their service. If you do, $2 for the first bag and $1 for each subsequent bag. If they are oversized, $2

Hotel Bus/Shuttle Driver – Give them two or three dollars. If there's a few of you or more, a dollar per passenger and a dollar per bag will work.

Comped Meal (Complimentary Meal) – 15% to 20% will do.

Bellman – $1 or $2 per bag. If they wait, take your bag from you upon arrival, and wait for you to check-in and go to your room with you, give them a bit more if you can afford it.

Taxis, Lyfts and Ubers – As mentioned elsewhere in this book, don't take taxis if you can get an Uber or a Lyft. That's not your question though. 20% here is a nice tip, even if it's a taxi. If they're hustling you to bring you somewhere else, you shouldn't give them anything.

You've hit the jackpot! – 1% for the smaller amounts ($1,000 or so) and 0.5% if they are a bit larger. I haven't hit this jackpot yet so this is what I hear.

Valet Parking Attendants – $2 or $3.

Front Desk Clerk/Receptionist – Try the $20 trick for a complimentary upgrade. Basically, you're sandwiching a $20 between your credit/debit card and your id at check-in and asking if there are any complimentary upgrades available. Some folks believe that the best time to try this is 5 pm to 6 pm (for me, it's worked at night-time), and if you have a birthday, anniversary, etc, to mention at the same time, all going well, they might just be able to take care of you. I received a HUGE basket of fruits, chocolate, and snacks for my birthday from the Mirage one time.

Room Service – it's often built-in with a service charge on your bill. If not, 10 to 15% is more than enough.

Cocktail Service/Bartender – A dollar per drink, more if you like, or 15% to 20% of the bill if you can. If the experience is good, treat them likewise, but 15% to 20% should do the job.

Buffet – $2 to $3 if you're on your own. If there are two of you $5 is cool between you. Buffet servers get to keep their own tips as far as I know.

# CHAPTER 2 - THINGS WORTH DOING AND/OR KNOWING ABOUT IN LAS VEGAS

This is basically a decent list that I have given to friends, and friends of friends of mine, that have asked me what they might consider doing in Las Vegas for some of their time there. There are all sorts here and it's quite random. I'll add to it in future books as I remember more, because there's never a dull moment in Las Vegas, unless you need one, and, well that's covered too.

Enjoy!

## Buffets:

Buffet at the Wynn is excellent – here's how I'd roll with this. There's buffet breakfasts, lunches and dinners. All different prices with dinner being the most expensive and breakfast the cheapest. You could go near the end of breakfast, so when breakfast is nearly over (cheapest option) then you'll get the lunch sitting (far more options) at the breakfast price or likewise do a VERY late lunch and you'll be in for the dinner food. It's cheeky for sure but do-able, and is it really wrong? I don't know. Ah, they'll get your money in other ways. If you're feeling guilty, you can give your server a nicer tip. You can use the MyVegas App to help with getting a discount on some of these. Wynn isn't on that app though but the Bellagio is, and I hear that that's one of the best ones, I haven't eaten at that buffet...yet. You can get these Apps on my site if you like.

## Night Clubs:

I don't really go to them as often these days, so I'm not best placed to advise, but I'll tell you what, I loved Blush at the Wynn, that was a very pretty boutique club, but it's gone.  There are tons of clubs in Vegas. Tryst at the Wynn was excellent but that's gone a while now too and was replaced by Intrigue. Marquee at Cosmo is very cool and over many levels. You could go there and you're going to enjoy it! Drai's was fun (initially I wasn't keen, but it was actually a really good spot for sure, and it's all been done up since I was last in it) as was Jet at the Mirage, fun! I'm going to stop for a moment, this isn't my best area. I'd be far better at bars and dive bars than clubs. I'll get advice from the locals for you on what's currently hot and what's not and put it on the site. Just to say though, if you're going to a club, get there during the day to put your name down on the list.

**Site Seeing:**

Go to the top of the Eiffel Tower at Paris, that's fun! You could eat at Mon Ami Gabi while you're there.

**For Concerts or Shows:**

Well, you'll get great deals here on the site or use Tix4Tonight on the Strip on the day itself.

**Bowling (if you're having a crash day and/or just want to have a few quiet drinks):**

Go to Brooklyn Bowl at the Linq and go to a gig or bowl. The bowling isn't cheap there, but they sometimes do offers in the free magazines for one hour free, normally on Tuesdays, I think. It's an experience to bowl there though, and especially if there's a gig on at the same time. You'd be bowling whilst the concert is on. I don't know if they always let people do this but they let me so they must do.

For much cheaper bowling try The Gold Coast (it's a little off the Strip and you'd get a cab there), $1.50 beers while you bowl and they'll bring you TGI's to eat while you bowl too if you want some.

Finally, on Bowling, for FREE Bowling, FREE Pool, FREE Video Games, go to The Nerd, 450 Fremont Street, 2nd Level (Downtown). It's not in the greatest of shape, the Bowling (they may have fixed it up since I was last there), but it's definitely a place to visit if you fancy spending time at pool, bowling and/or video games for free. It's a bar but I don't think they do food.

**Taxis/Cabs:**

Forget Cabs. I'm not going to advise you to get a cab when UBER and LYFT are in the main far cheaper and not to generalize, but the drivers tend to be friendlier as this is their business and they aren't working for a company. Forget about getting cabs, honestly, you don't need them.

**The High Roller:**

Highest observation wheel in the world, even higher than the London Eye. I lived a couple of minutes' walk from this. It's at the Linq. You will often find a great deal for this through my site. If you like to drink, take the free-bar option. Some people go absolutely baloobas drinking on this.

## If you love fancy cars:

Visit the Ferrari/Maserati Garage at the Wynn if you like fancy cars. 10 dollars in. The only joint Ferrari Maserati dealership in the States. There's more car stuff further on so keep reading!

## Las Vegas sign:

Visit the Las Vegas Sign and get some photos with it. I'd get a cab there and walk back if it's not too hot, stopping at Mandalay Bay on the way back. You can see the man-made beach in there and there's an Irish Bar there, so you can get refreshed with a drink. The bar is called RiRa. Lovely man from Kilkenny called Cyril works there. I only chatted with him on that one occasion but some people are unforgettable. Also, MIX bar/restaurant at Mandalay Bay is AWESOME for the view and make sure to check out the view from the ladies bathroom. A local showed me that. No funny business!

**I want to scare the Bejebus out of myself on...possibly, roller coasters? What do you reckon?**

The Big Apple Roller Coaster at New York New York. FUN!!! It actually goes through the casino at the end. Apparently, there's a hell of a new (a couple of years) roller coaster at Circus Circus now. Meant to be absolutely terrifying. I might not get on that one. I was on the old one at Circus Circus and survived after a good mental scare. I don't know if I was attached to it properly, and my friend laughing his arse off at my predicament didn't help, thus the mental stress. I hung onto those bars as if they were the holy grail itself. The New York New York one is very cool too. I've been on that one a few times now. I actually promised to become a Priest one time on a very dodgy wall of death ride. I didn't become a Priest. I don't know how to fix that promise. Ok then.

**AdventureDome at Circus Circus:**

While we're on the subject of Rollercoasters, this is really worth a visit. 5 (FIVE!) acres of indoor fun, enough said. You can get a full one-day pass or use it as part of choosing three activities in an MGM deal on my site or use the MyVegas app to get two for one on the Rollercoaster Ride at least. If you don't have this app, you know where you can get it. I don't want to keep mentioning my site! ;)

**I love Rock Music and I love Golf, and I might even get married to combine all three at once:**

Haha! This is a crazy combination of things but there you go. You should go to the Rio and the Kiss Mini-Golf, it's fun! That's the band Kiss, Gene Simmons, Paul Stanley. You do know them. They sing the song Crazy, Crazy Nights. Yeah, you've definitely heard it. "People try to take my soul away, but I don't hear the rap that they all say. They try to tell us we don't belong, that's alright, we're millions strong. This is my music, it makes me proud, these are my people and this is my crowd. These are Crazy, Crazy, Crazy, Crazy Nights!" There you go, told you that you knew them. You don't have to get married there, but if you want too, a Gene Simmons lookalike will look after you. There are many celebrity lookalikes to marry you there. Not to get married to you, to marry you like a priest or minister would. Deals for this, you know where.

**But, but, BUT! Who are these people Shane? Rock and Golf? I'm not a Rock Music fan. I love Golf though, AND I love the Twilight Zone. Again, I'm not a Rock fan.**

There's something for everyone of course! Well, you can go to Bally's for Twilight Zone Mini-Golf, can't you then? It's open 365 days a year, it's $11.95.

**Ziplines:**

At the Rio and there's one at Fremont (Downtown), and at the Linq... savage fun I reckon... ashamed to say that I haven't done either of them yet (money was needed for other things) but that's Las Vegas, you could live there for 2 years and not experience a quarter of it.

**Pub Crawl (Bar Hopping):**

If you want to do a pub crawl, forget the Strip, get yourself to Fremont (Downtown – Old Vegas) and try the zip line and all the bars. You'll love the Strip but this SHOULDN'T BE MISSED...the bars to visit... Park, Oak & Ivy, Bin 702, The Nerd, Corduroy, The Griffin, Atomic, Commonwealth, Gold Spike (make sure to go out the back of here) and Hogs and Heifers. Hennessey's up there is an Irish bar and that often has great deals. When you're back on the Strip or thereabouts, try Dino's, Ellis Island and Double Down. All definitely worth a visit.

## Dive Bars:

Worth visiting for sure are Dino's, Double Down, Velveteen Rabbit (all craft beers in Velveteen). There are more

## Late-night eating:

Well, you can do this nearly anywhere but I love Peppermill, just up from Encore for late-night grub. I used to go here a bit. Real old-style American Diner. Cocktails at 5 in the morning, and an awesome open fireplace to sit around and have a drink and/or food if you go in and to the left. Really nice fire, like being transported in time really.

The Secret Pizza Place is a great spot too (at the Cosmopolitan), for a couple of lovely slices of delicious Pizza and maybe even some excellent Cannoli. That shouldn't set you back more than about $15. Well worth it, this one.

And Tacos El Gordo just up past Encore on the way to the Strat. That's open until 4 am. Gorgeous Tacos! Really good! ☺

You are sorted.

## A cool place to eat with a bit of history:

There's a restaurant just parallel to the Strip near the High Roller called Battista's. I've eaten there a number of times now. It was minutes' walk away. The mob and the rat pack used to eat there and hold their meetings there. It's slightly hidden away, slightly, and most tourists might not even hear of it. Being honest, the food isn't the same as Italian food as I know it, but that doesn't mean that it's not very tasty and I really enjoy it. This place, so cool. Sinatra and all the lads. Plus, UNLIMITED wine with your dinner. There's a dive bar beside this too (I like the dive bars) called Stage Door. Cheap as chips! $1 beers and $1 hot dogs

## Stripburger and Chicken:

Visit Stripburger and Chicken, opposite the Wynn for $3 beers between 4 and 7 and 10 to close, and get the fried pickles with ranch too, unreal. Lots of great food here, great cocktails, sitting outside in the open air. I love it there, plus some of the nicest people I've met in life work here.

**Beer Lover:**

If you're down at the Linq get into Yardhouse if any of you love beer. 168 taps of all different beers. Great happy hour on food too. Look for the reverse happy hours at places too. These normally start at 9 or 10 pm to close. There are many other places serving many craft beers and own brew also in Las Vegas. I've made a nice list of deals for booze for you at the end of the book.

**Amusement Park:**

Visit Circus Circus for an amusement park and maybe have a steak in the Steakhouse while there. It's really old, a nice steak, pricey ...ish, but not too pricey. Why are steaks so expensive in Las Vegas? I mean, it could easily be said that we've got the best beef in the world in Ireland, and it's far cheaper. Don't tell me "oh, I thought the UK had the best beef". Most of their beef is exported to them from Ireland so there you have it. I'm not talking Kobe here, I'm talking steak that's actually affordable with the average industrial wage. Anyway, I've gone slightly off-topic here and trying to get away from eating meat so possibly shouldn't be encouraging you.

Pretty nice amusement centre in New York New York too.

Spielberg's GameWorks (which I loved) has moved from the Strip to Town Square (about a mile from Mandalay Bay). You can get a free shuttle from Planet Hollywood and Tropicana.

There's also meant to be a great weekend Amusement Park at Adventure Canyon which is in Primm, 40 miles south of Vegas. I haven't been to this one.

**Cowboys and/or Line Dancing:**

If you like country music crossed with rock and you like Cowboys, there's Stoney's at Town Square. Excellent though. Cowboys and Cowgirls drinking there. Line Dancing. Mechanical Bull. A locals spot. Sunday nights will be fun, from 7 pm, no cover, wells, wine, and draft beers $4.

**SHOPPING:**

The Euro is brutally bad right now versus the dollar and has been for a good while now. A Euro should really get you about $1.30, that's probably about par (and I think that's the shopping basket theory) but it's been low since the Greek issues and possibly before that. Anyway, Fashion Show Mall for shopping opposite the Wynn. Caesars' Forum Shoppes. Miracle Mile and so many more. For BARGAINS ...Las Vegas premium outlets, great shopping, MAKE sure to sign up at www.premiumoutlets.com first and print off vouchers and/or download their app, you'll save a fortune. DO THIS BEFORE YOU LEAVE FOR LAS VEGAS.

Visit the food court in the Fashion Show Mall if you're shopping and hungry, or go to Stripburger and Chicken... it's beside it.

**REALLY CHEAP (in price) FOOD and a great place for own brew and Karaoke:**

Ellis Island (was the Casino nearest to my apartment) for $9 Steak Dinner, starter and beer. It's an older casino. Many locals go here. The food and booze are great value, plus they brew their own. The staff are all lovely, those that I've chatted to. More about Ellis Island coming up later in the book.

**I'm not from the U.S. Shane, and electronics are more expensive in my country, any advice?**

Fry's Electronics for electronic stuff. Great deals for laptops, tablets, cameras etc. Sign up on frys.com to their email exclusives and you'll see. It's down close to Town Square. You might go to Brio for a feed while you're there, nice food! Fry's have amazing deals on Black Friday. Got myself a touch-screen laptop here before for $400 one Black Friday, really high spec and it was $1,200 in most other places. There's food also in

Fry's itself, and they do specials, but it's not the Brio standard which is fair enough as Brio is a restaurant and their own knowledge of laptops and tablets etc. most likely won't be as good as Fry's. If you're an Apple dude or dudette, you can become satisfied at Fashion Show Mall on the Strip opposite The Palazzo.

## Nine Fine Irishmen:

Are there? Haha, it's the Irish Boozer in New York New York. Apparently, it was brought over from Ireland brick by brick. It's nice. Walk right through it and you're on the Strip eating and drinking. Good Irish band there. They've got a decent shepherd's pie (should be called cottage really, as it's beef). Other good Irish bars to visit are RiRa at Mandalay Bay and McMullan's up opposite The Orleans.

## Terrace Point Cafe:

Don't leave Vegas without going to Terrace Point Cafe in the Wynn, sitting outside, and having Tomato Bisque Soup with sourdough bread and cheese while sitting out people watching at the pool. That's nice comfort food, especially if you have a hangover and its wintertime.

**More Scary Rides:**

Go to the Stratosphere (North End of Strip) and go on some of the rides. They will raise the hairs on your neck. I did ALL of these, pissed as a fantastic fart with a 70-year-old man from Birmingham in England. We tore the absolute backside out of it that night on the jar! That was some drinking. Great fun!

**Bellagio Fountains and FRENCH FOOD (MON AMI GABI):**

ON YOUR LAST NIGHT AT ABOUT 7:30 PM, good time for dinner. YOU'LL NEED TO BOOK THIS – HIGHLY RECOMMENDED. If you're booking, you can do it at the door or call them, make sure to ask for a seat on the patio, although I believe that they are first come first served. Have dinner in Mon Ami Gabi at Paris in the evening, sit outside and watch the Bellagio water show, amazing. Also, this could easily be the start of a romantic night out if you're with your partner. You can read more about Mon Ami further on. I love this spot.

**Seafood and Steak (for deeper pockets or a special occasion):**

I'd also highly recommend the food at Joe's at Caesars Forum Shoppes. Incredible! Oysters Rockefeller there was magnificent. Seafood and Steak.

## Almost Endless List of Food:

In the Caesar's Forum Shoppes there's also the Cheesecake Factory. Always……ALWAYS worth a visit.

## Mexican Food (relaxing sit-down meal or happy hour for food and drinks)

El Segundo Sol opposite the Wynn at Fashion Show Mall. Excellent Mexican food at a very fair price. I love it here. I-LOVE-IT-HERE.

## Mirage Volcano (Free show)

Yeah, a volcano erupts nightly at the entrance to The Mirage (Steve Wynn's second hotel in Las Vegas and the first hotel-casino in the world to turn over $1 million a day) and it's very cool! It's at 8, 9 and 10 in the evening on Fridays and Saturdays and it's at 8 and 9 in the evening other days. You can actually feel the heat of the Volcano, no messing!

## 107 Sky Lounge (Dinner, possibly romantic, with a serious view.

A serious view, actual view, not a serious view towards marriage, (that's up to you, and that's not to be forced)

Up high in The Strat, there is the cool bar-restaurant with a view that's very hard to beat. Up here, you'll be in the highest building in Western America and at one of its highest points. This would be another ace place to bring a romantic partner. They have a brilliant happy hour (the food is fantastic) and it's from 4pm – 7pm with 50% off cocktails and appetizers

## Fall of Atlantis Show at Forum Shops (Free)

The Myth of Atlantis recreated! This free show runs Sunday through Thursday every hour on the hour from 11 a.m. to 11 p.m. and Friday and Saturday every hour on the hour from 11 a.m. to midnight. You're beside the Cheesecake Factory here. Go in for a feed, it'd be rude not to.

## Lake of Dreams (free show at Wynn)

This free show I love! You can only see this inside Wynn Las Vegas. Lake of Dreams is spectacular. Music and imagery created by thousands of stunning holographics and puppetry. Inside the resort, take the circular escalator from Parasol Up and you'll see the dazzling shows that happen on and in front of the 40-foot waterfall and pine-topped mountain. You might have a sneaky one at Parasol Down whilst watching it. I love that frog in the show, you really need to see it to believe it. The show runs every half an hour (30 mins) from 8pm to 12:30am each night. Also, they have the Frog on some of the games on the Wynn Slots App that you can play to get rewards of free nights at the Wynn. You should download this for sure. That can save you hundreds and actually, a thousand and more depending on the nights you go for. DO IT!  Honestly though! I'm saying this for your benefit. There's a link in the "APPS" section on my site.

## Visit The Venetian (Gondolas and Haircuts, but there's so much more!)

If you want to feel like you might be in Venice. Go on a Gondola if you like. Very nice hotel. Lucky enough to have stayed here a couple of times. There's a great barbershop here, where a man in his 60-ties I reckon he was (he had a shop of his own years ago on the West Side of Vegas, I think he said to me, but he closed it and so works here now), he cuts hair. You'd be in a big barber shop all on your own (there's only one chair from memory) with him. It's called "The Art of Shaving". I think it's owned now by Proctor and Gamble or a company like that. Nice spot for a haircut though and not extortionately priced for the experience. On haircuts, one of my best friends, we were staying in the Wynn at the time, he got his haircut at the Wynn. I think it cost him $100 or so and his hair was short anyway, but he'll maintain to this day that it was the greatest haircut he ever had. I think the head massage played a part!

## The Bellagio Conservatory and Botanical Garden (Free)

This is next to the lobby in the Bellagio. Well worth a visit.

## See Real Flamingos! At the Flamingo (Wildlife Habitat). (Free)

I've seen these dudes sleeping, nuts! They were sleeping standing up and on one leg! I really didn't know that they did this. Apparently, it's to conserve body heat. Anyway, visit them! They're lovely! The Wildlife Habitat is open from dawn to dusk with Pelican feedings at 8:30 am and 2 pm daily and they also have Swans, Ducks, Koi Fish and Turtles.

## Circus Acts at Circus Circus! (Free)

The world's largest permanent circus, highlighting the centre stage of the Carnival Midway daily. Performances starting at 11:30 a.m. daily.

## Listen to (and dance to, if you want) Free Live Music and experience Viva Vision Light Show at Fremont Street

Runs each hour 6 pm to 1 am and is six minutes long. The Viva Vision Light Show video screen is 1,500 feet long, 90 feet wide and suspended 90 feet above

Fremont Street's renowned pedestrian mall, lined by iconic casinos and hotels. Music featured includes The Killers, Linkin Park, Green Day, Imagine Dragons, The Who and Tiesto. There were also Free Shows this year by very popular artists including Good Charlotte (May 24th), Nelly (June 15th), Sugar Ray (June 29th), Cheap Trick (August 24th), The Wallflowers (August 30th), Smash Mouth (28th September), all 2019.

**Crash Day in Hotel, need booze, food, maybe some medication for my poor head and stomach.**

Cool, use Instacart.com, Drizly.com or Getswill.com. For food, Postmates.com, Grubhub.com and Doordash.com or Instacart.com

**I want to play video games**

Go to Gameworks at Town Square. 6587 Las Vegas Blvd S, Ste 117. Or, go to Midway at Circus Circus, they've lots too. There are video games also at New York New York where the Big Apple Roller Coaster is.

**I'd love to see some Ice Hockey!**

Las Vegas has a team! They're called the Vegas Golden Knights, they play in the Pacific Division and at the new T-Mobile Arena. They started playing in 2017. They made the Stanley Cup finals in their first year but lost out over 5 games to Washington Capitals. The tickets aren't that cheap. The Golden Knights' mascot is a Gila monster.

## I really love Superhero films

Well, thanks for sharing. There are some good ones! You can get your photo taken with many superhero look-alikes on the Strip. How they cope with the heat in those suits, I'm going to find out. Also, there's Marvel Avengers S.T.A.T.I.O.N. it's an interactive and educational exhibit bringing visitors in the world of The Avengers. You can even try on Iron Man's suit and take it for a spin via virtual reality. There are 2 for 1 offers if you're staying in Treasure Island where this is located. I'll look for more offers for you.

## I'm keen to go Karting

Grand, there's indoor Karting over beside the Palms. Pole Position Raceway at 4175 S Arville St #100

**I want to propose to my darling with a message on a giant screen and tie them down to me forever and ever, and never let them get away. I'm very serious about this Shane, as you can probably tell. There is to be no escape for them! This IS the one! Definitely, this is it! This is the one. This IS the oneeeeeee. The stars have aligned for me! My other five marriages were practice.**

Ok, to me, you sound a little stressed. To others, these feelings of yours might be very normal. I don't know you so I can only go by your words here. You might be best off getting a pet to start with, and some CBD oil (for both you and the pet, it's only fair, and check if your pet can take it first) but only after a course of relaxation therapy, and I should know, I've been quite stressed during life at times too. First thing, everything, everyone, changes, it's the way of the Universe, so what you want now, might not be what you want in the months or years to come. When you're in Vegas, regardless of how drunk you get, remember that sentence because it's very easy to just jump on the rollercoaster, and maybe not be properly buckled in mentally. That wouldn't be good for your partner nor you. It could save you a lot of money, heartbreak and potential hardship. Embrace change, it makes life much easier. You might change. He, she, might change. It might last forever, it might not, don't be too uptight about it. Just know your rollercoaster as best you can is basically my advice. If you know your rollercoaster well enough, marry them, if you want, I'm not going to be responsible for you, they're your rollercoaster, I've enough going on. Maybe someday I'll marry my rollercoaster, maybe not. I'd be their rollercoaster too of course, so who knows, they might not enjoy my twists, turns, and my sudden loop the loops. Never say never, except to Hitler and Stalin obviously, and that Grand-daughter of Mussolini who quite possibly isn't that fond of Jim Carrey. I'm not sure how marriage advice became part of this list but screw it, it's Vegas, anything could possibly happen and does happen and ought to be addressed, or not, it depends. Also, I'm not one to advise you on any "tying down" business, I've never indulged, so just know your knots like any good scout would (in case you're left high and dry, and emotionally or physically in knots), and then off up to Fremont with you. A simple text message on their giant "Viva Vision" costs a "mere" $500. They can also spice things up for you with a photo or video. If you're interested in this, you can get in touch and I'll help you out and you'll be married in no time at all, with all the pleasure and the pain that can accompany this arrangement for you. Be open to both (these are undeniable) and you'll have a great chance at a long-lasting marriage. This advice comes free of charge and is possibly just useless, and certainly not legally binding.

**I want to terrify the living daylights out of myself and/or see my loved ones in a state of discomfort**

Because believe me, you will if you go on the rides at the top of The Strat (formerly known as The Stratosphere), these are the highest thrill rides in the U.S. Big Shot, Insanity and X-Scream are the ones to do. The admission to the Tower and to do these three rides is $35 during the week. It's pricier at weekends. I'll look for a deal for this one for you too. I did these quite drunkenly. I thought I might meet my maker that night but fortunately didn't. I've more to do in this world yet, clearly, but I constantly think that I'm about to die on these things, it's bloody ridiculous. Need to sort this out. If you're staying in The Strat, it's cheaper for you. Also, the Sky Jump is here! This is basically jumping from the top of the building attached to a wire and you fall all the way to the ground. I'm going to give that a go someday. I didn't have the money for it the last time. You can include this with "Unlimited Tower and Rides" for $144.95. Visit my site for these, or don't, that's fine too, I'll leave that with you.

**I'm being brought to Las Vegas but in truth, I'm a beach person. I don't want to go.**

My heart bleeds for you, but really, if this is a complaint, it's going to fall on deaf ears. First word problems my friend, and you're being brought to undoubtedly one of the fun-est places on this planet. If you need the beach, and if this is an obvious connection to nature that you're hopefully displaying here, and I'm being not so nice with my answer, I apologise and have a recommendation for you. You should stay in Mandalay Bay. There's a man-made beach there. It's an 11-acre aquatic playground where you can catch the sun, swim or splash. You can ride tides in the wave pool or just flow along with the Lazy River. Non-Mandalay Bay guests are welcome to Mandalay Bay Beach if they pay. Valid Monday – Thursday. Adults are $20, Kids 4-16 years old are $10, Kids 3 and under are complimentary. There are blackout dates on this.

**I want to Sky-Dive, but not from the real Sky. Listen, Shane, basically, I've heard that there's indoor Skydiving. Please enlighten me.**

Well I can help you with more knowledge on this, but actual enlightenment in general, that's a different thing and apparently, if a person seeks it, they don't get it, but that's enough spirituality. The Sky Diving is up close to Encore. For $75 you can have a "A LEARN TO FLY" experience includes all equipment, training, instructor, and 2 minutes of tunnel time for one participant. For $99, it's the same deal but 5 minutes. There are group offerings also, for example for up to 5 participants, for $300 there's a 10-minute flight deal.

**I'm quite a refined lady and I was meant to be brought to Paris, France, but turns out my louser (this is an Irish-ism, it means "a mean, unpleasant, or contemptible person") boyfriend is bringing me to Las Vegas instead. I'm not sure whether to be happy or sad or will I just leave in short order?**

Nice to have someone Irish here, coolio. You're funny! Be happy! As often as possible in this life. Your boyfriend likes randomness, lights, great vibes and you'll get all of this with almost one million people per week going to LV for a holiday/vacation. Las Vegas will be one of the most unique places you'll ever visit! I've been in both cities numerous times (Paris is only 90 minutes or so from Dublin but as you're Irish, you'll know this) and they are both extremely different experiences BUT there is a bit of Paris in Las Vegas and funnily enough it's called "Paris Las Vegas". There's an Eiffel Tower (1/2 size of the real McCoy) there, an Arc De Triomphe (2/3 the size of the real one), a lovely French restaurant called Mon Ami Gabi (you should go there and sit out on the patio and watch the Bellagio water show in the evening, or go for Brunch and have ham and cheese crepes or a croque monsieur, plus they do incredible mash!). It's not Paris France, but it's the next best. You can go up the Eiffel Tower in a glass elevator, it's fun and a great view. Enjoy it though, he can bring you to the "real" Paris another time if you haven't left him. Even if you have, you might rekindle it all for a trip to France, but enjoy Vegas, it's very different for sure!

**I want to see waxed celebrities.**

Whaaaaaat? Hang on. Oh, ok. You're talking waxworks celebrities, aren't you? I'll go with that, otherwise I'm not going to know how to help you, I'm not really moving in those circles. If it's in fact celebrities made of wax, you can go to Madame Tussauds at the lovely Venetian. They've got Gaga and Elvis there. Alan from the Hangover too.

**Unlike the punter who asked you before about "indoor skydiving", I want to do the real thing Shaner. Can I?**

Yes, you can. The good people at "GoJump" can take care of you. It's a tandem jump. The height you'll leap from 15,000 MSL (Mean Sea Level). There are additional charges for folks over 220 pounds which is 15.7 stone and just shy of 100 kilos (99.79kg).

**I'd like to see the Strip from a Helicopter.**

One flying in the air? Obviously. DOS - Deal on site (we'll call it from here on). Well, there's a deal for a 12 to 15-minute flight where you'll get a good view of it,

I'm told. I've been in a helicopter before, and once is enough for me, for now anyway.

**That waxworks celebrities thing interests me, but so does the High Roller and I love the jar/booze/sauce. Got anything that might interest me?**

Yeah, ok then! Let me get this right, you want to do some drinking, see Madame Tussauds and go on the High Roller. Right, there's a great DOS where you can get admission to Madame Tussauds Las Vegas with 30 minutes of unlimited open bar at Madame Tussauds Las Vegas' The Hangover Bar, and admission to High Roller with 30 minutes of unlimited High Roller Happy Half Hour Anytime. This is a great deal. I've heard of lots of people having at least 6 and 7 drinks on the 30 minutes in the High Roller and even that of a lady drinking 12 drinks in the 30 minutes. That's a drink every 2 and a half minutes, WOW! I'm a big enough guy at 6 foot 4, and I was a very talented drinker in that I could take a lot (a lot!) and stay fairly sober (sometimes), or at the very least find my way home safely. I think that that level in such a short time frame, that level might knock me into the middle of next week and affect my organs in a not so mega way. I might need to experiment again sometime, but bloody hell, I wouldn't look forward to that hangover. Please don't drink 12 drinks in 30 minutes at this, as you'll already have had an open bar just before at Madame Tussauds. Don't die on us!

**I like big butts and I cannot lie. Actually, that's not what I meant to say, I do like the song though, reminds me of a friend of mine. I'll tell you again Shane, in private obvs. What I meant to say was, I love cars, are there any fancy ones to see?**

Haha, funny! I've got a great friend who we (very quietly) called Sir Mix-a-lot, so this is not new to me. That being said, let's deal with cars as I can't advise you on this penchant of yours. There's a Ferrari Maserati dealership at the Wynn if you come up Trumps with your gambling and wish to make a purchase with your winnings, or you can visit it for $10 I think it was. Oh, and there's this! An admission package for one to Hollywood Car Museum and Liberace Garage for under $20. These are cars that graced the big and small screens including the DeLorean from Back to the Future and the Knight Rider car from, well, Knight Rider. Was that car not called Kitt? That was what I always thought. Maybe that was just the voice of the car. Also, there is the Chitty Chitty Bang Bang car, Herbie from "The Love Bug." the A-Team stunt van too. If you're a James Bond fan, you can see a motorcycle, Lotus submarine car, and even an Osprey 5 Hovercraft. The Batmobile from the Michael Keaton era and the neon green Mitsubishi Eclipse driven by Paul Walker in the "The Fast and the Furious" are also part of the collection. DOS (Deal/s on site)

**I'd just love to be picked up from my hotel on the Strip in a Military Humvee and to go shooting a machine gun.**

Sure thing. Give this a go... Battlefield Vegas might just be the thing for you. DOS.

**My partner's drinking is really getting to me. He drank an entire bottle of Fireball last night and so, so many beers. My God, it was insane. How we weren't thrown out of places I don't know. He's loud when he drinks. I need some time away from them and I'd love to have a Spa day or at least a few hours there.**

Ah, the aul Fireball, nice! Haven't had it in so long! That's a gateway back to drinking for sure. Right, the Spa at the Wynn and the Spa at the Venetian/Palazzo are both excellent options for you. I've been in both and enjoyed each very much. I was loud with the booze too. My hearing isn't mega (in the opinion of others, being honest, I think I've got more than my fair share of mumblers in my life) and I just couldn't hear right when I drank so my voice got louder, and well, that's my excuse and I'm sticking to it.

**Shane, I'd love to have my dinner as high as possible in Las Vegas.**

As high up as possible, yeah? Is that what you meant? Ok, I'm going with that. 844 feet in the air, the "Top of the World" Restaurant at the Strat and it REVOLVES! They have a special which comes in at under $83 per person (for Sunday to Thursday, you must also buy a beverage on top), with a great 4 course meal with a choice of various items and you could be eating Lobster Bisque Soup, Maryland Lump Crab Cake, Filet Mignon and Shrimp or Salmon and Shrimp, finished off with Salted Caramel Creme Brule or a Sorbet Trio. That menu is subject to change clearly, and it's an award-winning restaurant. In my mind, this is good value especially if you're planning a romantic night out. If I've read this incorrectly, and I may have done, you know that you can go to any number of dispensaries in Las Vegas now as it's all legal. They'll look after you for sure! Back to food though… A less expensive option would also be in the Strat, going for the happy hour for food and drinks at 107 Sky Lounge. This is really great value and delicious!

**I'd love to see Elvis.**

Well, we're told that he's shuffled off this mortal coil (or maybe not) but you've got other options. There's Big Elvis at Harrah's Piano bar, he's there at 2 pm, 3:30pm and 5 pm on Monday, Tuesday, Thursday and Friday. It's a free show.

There's a great Elvis (called Gary) at Ellis Island in the Karaoke bar. He's a really nice guy. He performs every Friday and Saturday in the Village Pub there at 5 pm. Go and have some food there (it's inexpensive and tasty, the booze too) and watch him. I enjoy this show. Also, Gary deals Blackjack in the casino at Ellis, 6 pm Tuesday to Thursday.

There are other Elvises (three Elvises? Hahaha, if you've watched Father Ted, you'll get this joke) and a top man who played Elvis at Legends in Concert both on the Strip and worldwide, he was even in Ireland which is cool. I met this lovely man one night as he was my Uber driver. He sang Elvis songs to me and my friend in the car. My friend had lost their phone, he found it, found me through Facebook as he didn't know whose phone it was, and brought it back the next morning. Such a total gentleman. If you'd like him to pick you up and bring you from the airport to your hotel or elsewhere, contact me, I owe this man for his honesty, plus he's a good guy.

**Are there any street parties in Vegas?**

Yep! There's a free one at Carnaval Court at Harrah's on the Strip. There are flair bartenders, live DJ, live bands, and it's from midday to 3 am each day. It's not quite Rio but it's fun, go!

## Shane, I really love insects.

Ok, that's random but cool. I enjoyed Arachnophobia, the film, but you're probably on another level here and that's cool. If you visit Container Park at night, there is a GIANT Praying Mantis there. It shoots out fire which is very cool. What's even cooler is that this isn't at a set time and the controller decides when it operates. They've been known to let it rip upon unsuspecting passers-by (let the Mantis rip, not wind, I've no knowledge of the controller's movements regarding that. "The "Controller", what a great name. "I....AM... THE.... CON-TROLL-ER". That's in an 80s version of a future robot voice). Fun times! Whilst up there, go into the place, visit Container Park, it's very cool and if you've got kids with you, they'll love it. Apparently, in some parts of Africa, it's considered good luck if a Praying Mantis lands on you, so there you go. If this one happens to land on you (there's no reason to think that it will), it's goodnight Vienna for you, I would imagine, it's BIG. It is Vegas after all!!

### I loved the Osmonds. Are Donny and Marie still in Vegas?

Yes! Until November 16th this year (2019) at the Flamingo. It's all over then, but maybe they'll run a show at a different casino? Very possible.

# CHAPTER 3 - 32 VALUABLE LAS VEGAS HOTEL BOOKING TIPS

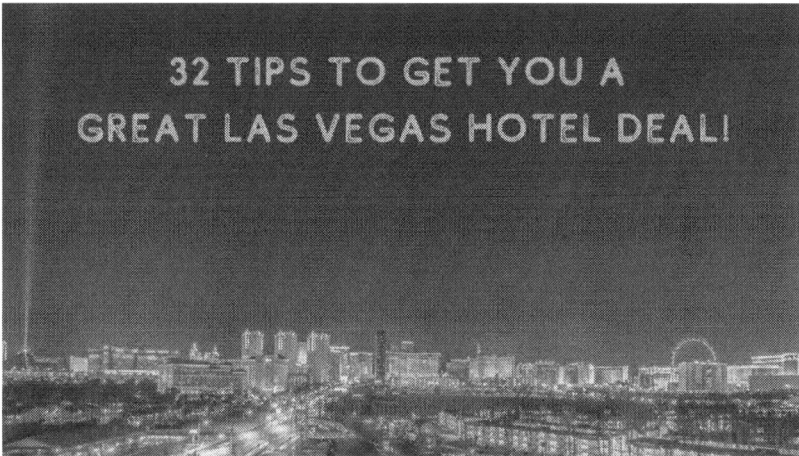

There's a bit of reading for you here, but all in all, valuable for you. If you just want to know how you might earn a free stay at the Wynn, you can just go to the end of this chapter to number 32. If you don't know the Wynn, you should make it your business to, trust me. In the words of Larry David, it's pretty, pretty good. It's actually more impressive than that Larry, it's totally swish! Ok, you've reading to get on with, enjoy it, and I'll get out of your way.

## 1. The cheapest time of the year to visit

December. I often do. The negatives first. It's not ideal pool weather, some shows won't be running, some casinos will be dolling themselves up, it'll be quieter, but with all that, you'll get great attention from staff as they have more time etc., A few positives for December...it's got lovely Christmas-ey things going on (ice-skating at The Cosmopolitan, often free warm apple cider at The Venetian), the National Rodeo Finals are on (room rates can sometimes be higher on those dates in comparison to other December dates with the Rodeo on, but often not really from experience, and you'll still get very decent deals as it's December), you could do your Christmas shopping in the outlets, and when you're leaving Las Vegas in December, it's a lovely feeling to be going home for Christmas. I could go on and on. Just before Thanksgiving is also a time that you'll get great rates. New Year's Eve is a no-no pricewise, for me anyway. July and August often have very good room rates too as it's so hot at this time.

## 2. Cheapest days to stay

IF you stay Sunday and check-out on or before Friday, you'll get the BEST rates on rooms. The weekends (Friday and Saturday nights) will nearly always be more expensive, often far more. If you are staying longer, say 12 nights (I often do, and it's not nearly enough for me), you should only have two of the twelve nights as a Friday and Saturday night, and you'll save significantly.

## 3. Check the convention dates

Las Vegas is a convention capital, so rooms are going to be more expensive when the bigger ones are on, even if there are over 151,000 rooms in the city.

## 4. The universally HATED resort fees!

Filthy, filthy dirty words these. When I first started going to Las Vegas, this wasn't a thing at all. I don't like the practice, not at all, but it's here in full-flow and it's pretty much unavoidable except in certain resorts IF you take a very expensive upgrade. If you're booking a room and the resort fee isn't mentioned, the likelihood is that the first thing you're going to know of it is when you get hit with it as you check out of the hotel. There are very, very, few Las Vegas hotels without the resort fee and the charge are from (these figures are WITHOUT tax and PER day) $8.95 (El Cortez) to $45 (Venetian and Palazzo, beautiful luxury 5 Star). So, in practice, if you're staying five nights at The Venetian or The Palazzo (both incredibly beautiful resorts at the $45 side on the resort fee), you'll be paying $225 in resort fees plus tax when you checkout.

The resort fee generally covers:

Free internet access, a daily newspaper, Free boarding pass printing and free local phone calls. Sometimes gym or spa access. To note, and for fairness, both The Venetian and The Palazzo (sister hotels) offer two guests access to Canyon Ranch SpaClub (it's really top notch!) as part of the resort fee, the other bonuses just mentioned, and one two-for-one drink coupon for well drinks, domestic beer, or wine at any casino bar excluding the pool decks. So, this resort fee has positives but I'm out. I'm not happy with this practice as I don't think it's fair.

Here's a trick that can "often" help you avoid resort fees AND stay in a swanky place. HomeAway.Com, if you book on here, you can get a room at MGM Signature, Palms Place, Trump International or Vdara (all high-end hotels) amongst others and again, often without resort fees. These are owner-listed condos.

Again, there's a way to stay at the Wynn Las Vegas and not pay resort fees. If you weren't reading the top half of this page you won't have known. You can just jump down to Number 32.

Read the first couple of lines of the next paragraph too as this can help avoid fees too, but no guarantees folks!

## 5. $20 trick for an upgrade?

If you haven't heard of this, let me explain this. Some will use a $50, but not totally necessary unless you've got deeper pockets (BUT, and please let this register, if you're staying a few days or more, it's to help you, I have heard of resort fees being waived with this. Could you be this lucky? Maybe!). You've booked your room and you've arrived at the hotel. You were wondering if you'd see if there are upgrades available. You don't really want to pay full upgrade price of course and get it for free if possible (your $20 is a tip). All you do is ask the receptionist the question, "I was wondering if there were any complimentary upgrades available right now?" and while you're doing this, you've sandwiched a twenty in between your ID and your credit card which they'll have asked for to check you in. Make sure that it's partially visible at least. Sometimes it works, sometimes it doesn't. It depends on what they have really. Don't feel in any way awkward doing this. The receptionists are well used to it, it's normal practice, and it's certainly not frowned upon, and welcomed by most staff. They'll also possibly ask you if the money is for them. The best time to do this to give yourself the best chance is to check-in late in the evening when most of the guests have already checked in and/or on a Sunday night. IF they can't upgrade you, they most likely won't take your $20 or $50. I've no control over them (!), and people will be people of course! A little risk with potentially very comfortable rewards. You're in Vegas of course, might as well start with this gamble, if the airport slots didn't get you first, ha. I got an upgrade for a tenner one time. It was all the cash I had on me at that moment, I was only off the plane, and it was a Monday night, and not crazy busy. The upgrade came with a deal where if you didn't need your room cleaned, you get $10 credit for food each day that you don't avail of them. This was in the Westgate, the old Hilton where Elvis had his residency. Over the years more people saw Elvis perform there than anywhere else in the world, there's a fact-oid for you now.

## 6. Birthday/Special Occasion – Freebies?

If you are coming to Las Vegas for a special occasion, anniversary or birthday, or what have you, make sure that you inform the hotel when making your booking. You never know what they might surprise you with. I received an upgraded room (at no extra cost) AND a massive fruit and snacks basket from The Mirage for a birthday of mine, simply by putting a little note in with my booking. Thanks to The Mirage! I never forgot!

Oh yeah... apart from hotels and your birthday etc. sign up with restaurants in Las Vegas (if you're there for your birthday) and you might get a little surprise! I hear that Denny's will feed you for free on your birthday. There are others too that give you something.

I'll make a note of them as I find them and let you know through the site

## 7. Stay for FREE?

FREE rooms? I can think of four ways right now, two I'm not keen on myself for different reasons but plenty seems to be. I'll deal with them first.

The first being if you are interested in doing some gambling. I don't really gamble so I don't know the exact amount you need to gamble (I believe it's in the thousands from what I hear, and I also hear that it's not worth it unless you've got deep pockets and love gambling) or to win, and/or over which time period, so I can't and I won't advise you on that, except that if you're gambling, sign up in each resort for their players cards, make sure that you use them when you're gambling and spending money there on whatever you're buying, AND make sure to give them your postal address, you never know what surprises you'll get in the mail/post from them. Also, you'll need to focus on the hotel or the group of hotels in that chain. Plus, many hotels give you a little something free when you sign up for their players card. I'll get in touch with those that will be able to advise you properly on gambling for comps (rooms, dinner, show, drinks etc.) and get that info and hopefully some numbers for you. That'll be on the site. I'm just not very hot on gambling, I like to gamble, but very rarely, and also, there's so much more to do in Las Vegas for me, and anyway, I'm a Taurean. Again, though, for comped rooms, you really need to be gambling in the thousands from what I've been told.

The second one is if you're willing to sit through time-share presentations (I wouldn't be keen on doing it, you might. Again, might be for you, that's cool, I don't know why I'm even mentioning it as it's not for me but again, could certainly be for others depending on their journey in life. I'm not always great at saying no, so this option is not for me). You'll find plenty of these. In the Flamingo certainly.

Note: IF you do get a complimentary room (from the hotel/NOT the timeshare people), it's almost expected that you would tip $50.

Ok, those are two options that won't be for most people so what have I got for you? Ok, NOW...this is worth the money to you... there are apps that you can play on your smartphone or on Facebook which at times offer free rooms (you pay the resort fees on most, but not all) so that's definitely something that you can do. They offer deals for rooms, food, drinks, and entertainment. I'll explain this further in a bit. You SHOULD read it! Definitely

Oh, and here's a FOURTH method, it'll be for some and not for others, you can stay FREE if you are willing to be a House Sitter. You can register here...

www.trustedhousesitters.com

## 8. Cookie tracking

If you're doing an online search, clear your browser's cookies beforehand as otherwise, you "could" end up paying more as cookies help a site provider know what you're looking at/for and they might keep putting up the price. This is controversial I'm sure. Some say that it doesn't happen, others are adamant that it does. Doing this should safeguard you whether it actually does or doesn't. This is very easy to do and you should have this option under "Tools/History" in most browsers. If after doing this you see a really great rate, don't clear them again, the booking site may offer you an even lower one.

## 9. Choice of device when searching

Compare the price that you find on your laptop/desktop with the same site that you look up on your smartphone or mobile device. Often sites use a different system to update these prices so your luck could be in.

## 10. Promo codes!

I'm going to have these built into offers on the site but it's worth you knowing about if you're looking yourself. This is obviously a newer one but one that you should use regardless of what site you're using to book or order whatever it is. Promo Codes (promotional codes). Let's say that you're going to book online with The Mirage directly, then always, always, always, do a Google Search for "Mirage Las Vegas Promo Codes" and see what you can get. All you need to do is copy and paste them. Definitely something to do. You can do this with Walmart, BestBuy, any online site really, for your day to day online shopping. This is going to save you moolah for Vegas too remember? The less you spend day to day, the more you have to enjoy yourself with in Las Vegas!

## 11. Call the hotel after 6pm PST (Las Vegas time) and two other tricks

If you intend to book directly with the hotel, call them (even though online rates are often cheaper) after 6pm BUT know the online rates first. Also, dial the local hotel number and not the 800 numbers, and instead of asking for reservations, ask to speak with the manager, or the director of sales. They have the right to alter rates for you.

## 12. This one is just a general tip and not initially a money saver, but yes, possibly a money saver if you're willing, ah well...

This isn't really one that's going to save you money, but it will help you have a nicer time and its good advice based on experience. Pick a nice hotel, life is short. We never know how long we're here for. Be good to yourself, honestly, do. Do a little bit of research for yourself, or let me help you, see my site (I'm offering to find you deals with my own fingers!). You'd be very surprised how, for just a little bit more patience and a few dollars more (or maybe not even), you could change your idea from a 2 or 3-star hotel, to a 4 or even a 5-star hotel. You WILL spend quite a bit of time in your hotel, the hotel is a HUGE part of the experience, and you're going to Las Vegas where there are some of the greatest hotels in the world so you should really enjoy it! If you're not sure that you can get the deal, contact me. I'd like to help you. For sure! Or just download the Wynn Slots App from my site and you can earn a FREE Stay. For sure!

## 13. Slightly Off-Strip

Look at the "off-Strip" hotels including The Palms, Palms Place, Trump International (this is really only a few minutes' walk to the Strip in truth, and they run a free shuttle to the Wynn and Caesars Palace), Rio and the Hard Rock Hotel. These hotels (just mentioned off Strip) all run free (last time I looked) shuttles to the Strip and they are nearly always a fair bit cheaper to stay in. I've stayed in both Palms Place and Trump, beautiful hotels. More Condo-y than hotel, but very high standard. You will get good deals on these I'm fairly sure. Again, contact me if you need help.

## 14. Hotels WITHOUT a casino

Look at the "non-gaming" hotels including Vdara (maybe not as cheap as the next two), Palms Place and Trump International. Obviously, many will avoid Trump International due to many different reasons but I'm just here giving you options and I'm not getting involved in this. I've listened to too many arguments and none of it is helping people. There are good and bad people on both sides and unfortunately, politics and religion divide good people. I'm staying out of it. Peace and Love folks. Back to it, Palms Place and Trump International are cheaper than all the other 4.5 – 5-star hotels normally. If it's your first time going to Las Vegas, I'd leave these for another time (unless you don't want a casino in your hotel, then you could easily choose one of these) as staying on the Strip itself is a phenomenal experience. Vdara is on the Strip, and Trump International might as well be as it's so close to the Fashion Show Mall.

## 15. Low-Cost Hotels on the Strip

Low-cost hotel-casinos on the Strip (with great location) include Bally's, Flamingo, Linq and Harrah's. I've only rested in the Linq of these, and it was very acceptable and a fun place in the heart of it all, what with it being alongside Linq Promenade. I lived behind it a couple of times. These are all very central Strip but I can't tell you any more as regards the quality of the rooms bar the Linq. All very reputable, just to note. Off the Strip, Tuscany is different. Very comfy, no issues, some decent food, and it's quieter. Maybe for an older crowd Tuscany, I enjoyed it though.

## 16. Downtown is cheaper than the Strip

There are other ways, and you could certainly stay Downtown (Fremont). The rooms are substantially cheaper than most on the Strip, the food can cost less, and there is low-limit gambling. Super bars there too! A really great place to go pub crawling/bar hopping for sure! There are far better pub crawls (and cheaper) to be had Downtown than the Strip, things are just closer for a pub crawl and that's important. The Nugget (as the locals call it) or if you don't know it, The Golden Nugget, it's probably the fanciest of the hotels Downtown. It was Steve Wynn's first hotel-casino in Las Vegas (he built The Bellagio, The Mirage, Treasure

Island, sold them all to build Wynn in 2005, then Encore, two years later) so you'll know it's good!

## 17. Loyalty cards

You should join M-Life (you'll need to if you want to try and win free rooms and/or other freebies and discounted offers, that I'm going to tell you about as regards the MyVegas App. M-Life is the MGM Mirage Properties Reward Card. Bellagio Las Vegas, MGM Grand Las Vegas, Mandalay Bay Resort and Casino, The Mirage Las Vegas, Luxor Las Vegas, Excalibur Hotel and Casino, New York New York Hotel and Casino, Park MGM (formerly Monte Carlo) Las Vegas, and ARIA Las Vegas are all properties that you can claim discounts and get special deals from if you play My Vegas Slots. The App is free and I'll tell you more about it on the site (but please read on first as I'm going to get to it anyway, and there's more information for you that will help you besides this).

## 18. Another loyalty card

Also, join Caesar Rewards (formerly called Total Rewards) too, and earn rewards when you play, dine, shop or stay at their properties including Caesars Palace, Rio All-Suite Hotel & Casino, Harrah's Las Vegas, Planet Hollywood Resort & Casino, Paris Las

Vegas, Bally's Las Vegas, The Cromwell and Nobu Las Vegas.

## 19. Take someone's room!

Well not quite! You're not invading a room and chucking someone out! This is something quite novel and cool that you can do, and you'll be helping out the people that you purchase from. Buy someone's booking. This can of course be hit and miss as regards availability, and you'd need to be flexible with your dates. If your dates are somewhat open, go to RoomerTravel, and choose "Don't Miss A Deal" at the very top of the page. Type in Las Vegas, choose "anytime", and give them your email address. You will receive offers this way by email, from RoomerTravel for rooms that people have booked but can't stay on those dates. They are for rooms that can't be cancelled and can offer a discount of up to 74% at times, nice! Again, always compare these prices with the Hotel Tonight App, Trivago, Hotelscombined.com and have a look at my site too, as I might have found one for you that will beat it. Being honest, it's difficult to beat 74% off, but I'll be trying, and as I said, this can be hit and miss, of course they are dates that might not work with your plans, and they're not all 74% off, but up to 74% off. Definitely worth a look though.

## 20. AAA, Military, AARP

AAA, military or AARP members can often receive great discounts when booking hotels. With AARP membership (only $12 a year currently, 25% off the $16 year offer) you get access to discounts for travel (Hilton, Starwood, Wyndham), dining (Denny's, Outback Steakhouse), entertainment, and shopping. Anyone can join from most countries although they have no offer for Irish or UK residents to join right now. I'm going to contact them and ask why. They cover so many countries as regards their membership base so why Ireland and the UK aren't covered, I'm not quite sure. The membership fee really is a pittance for the discounts that you'll get.

## 21. Price-Matching

Some might not bother with this and that's cool. Each to their own. If you're want to book directly with a hotel, shop around on Trivago, Hotelscombined, Hotel Tonight, ebookers etc. first and give them a call to price-match the best one that you've found. They often will, as they will get paid immediately and won't have to wait on the third-party site that you might have booked with. This is advantageous to you if you have a player's card or if you intend to sign up for one.

## 22. Discounted e-gift cards

You can buy discounted e-gift cards, from Gift Card Granny etc. (these are gift cards that people received as presents/gifts and wish to sell on, they sell them at a discount) AND use these to book part or all your hotel etc. You can get them for all sorts of online stores, restaurants, car hire etc. so you can use these for more than your hotel booking in Las Vegas if you have a look around this site. So, once you've decided on who you're flying with, where you're staying etc, you can give a quick look on GiftCardGranny.Com to see if they have any offers for those that will give you the discount. You'd be surprised at how much you can save by paying with a discounted e-gift card.

## 23. Rent a home OR A BUS!

How about if you wanted to rent a home? This can be much cheaper if there are a few of you or more heading to Las Vegas, and of course you'll most likely dodge those poxy resort fees, which is a nice bonus and probably no parking fees either (for most places as these in the main are homes) if you're bringing or hiring a car. You can use HomeAway.Com (very similar to VRBO both being owned by the same parent company) for this and often they'll have condos in MGM Signature, Palms Place etc (top-notch places) at reduced prices that owners will rent them to you for. Of course, there are houses too. I saw a really cool "Downtown Fun Bus" offer, which for ONLY $100 per night, sleeps 6 adults and 2 children. It's a completely renovated 35' RV. Its resident address is at the Main Street Station Casino RV Park, on the North End of Fremont Street, and it's just a short walk across the street to so much that Vegas has to offer. To note, you don't get to drive it around. It stays there. The Main Street Station Casino RV park has a pool at the California Resort that you would have access to. It has 3 bunk-beds in the galley, and a queen-sized bed in the back bedroom. This comprises of 1 queen, 2 full, 2 twins, and 2 junior-sized beds. A full kitchen and bath with all the appliances and cooking utensils at your disposal. Plus, towels, linens, toiletries, etc... All the comforts and convenience of a hotel, but at a fraction of the cost. Now that's definitely for some people. I haven't been in the RV park, so that's all the knowledge I have on this particular offer. Sounds good to me. Always, always, stay safe in Las Vegas. Stick to the main streets. I hopefully don't really need to tell you this.

## 24. Be credit card savvy!

Be smart with your Credit Card. Check with your company, Mastercard, Visa, etc, or the bank you have the card with if this applies to you, to see if they offer discounts with the hotel that you've chosen or sites like hotels.com, trivago, ebookers, expedia.com/co.uk, etc.

## 25. Download this App!

GET THE HotelTonight App on my site. This is sweet. Hotel Tonight are given unsold rooms by hotels and they pass them onto you and I, at very often, super rates. Not many people in Ireland or the UK might be familiar with this app so I will explain it a bit further. You have nothing to lose by downloading it, and it really can save you money. This, and I can't state this strenuously enough, even if you're only using it as a comparison, as it's a wise step to compare this app for the hotel that you want with Trivago.com and Hotelscombined.com. You should ALWAYS check a few sites once you know the hotel that you want, and by checking the latter two against HotelTonight, you'll have covered multiple sites without maybe actually knowing it, as these are aggregator sites that will search the major booking engines for you. It's to protect you that I'd advise this. I WANT YOU TO SAVE MONEY! That's what I'm here for. Do I use CAPS too often? Haha! Sorry.

You can book using Hotel Tonight a full 100 days in advance and book a stay for as long as 14 days, and a week in advance for stays of up to 5 nights. If you use my code sdonnelly18 - you'll get €20 off your booking also, or whatever €20 is in your currency depending upon where you're reading this. If you're in dollars, it's going to be higher right now. Again, I'd always run my findings through Trivago.com also and Hotelscombined.com too though. Find your deal wherever you like and check the same property on those two anyway and I really can't see you going wrong.

Please ALSO note – Hotel Tonight bookings are NON-REFUNDABLE, so that's why I'd book it on the day itself (where possible) when I know that a flight interruption, or what have you, doesn't get in the way.

## 26. Business-focused hotels

You could stay in the business-focused hotels during the summer or at weekends when demand is less as regards business folks. The cost is often less too. So again, if you're going for let's say 12 days, only two of them need be Friday and Saturday nights, stay these two nights in the business focused hotels and stay the other 10 in two other places, 5 nights in each. A bit of moving around but in my opinion, fantastic, as it changes the holiday with each move AND you will make a saving, you've got really great options by being open to this.

## 27. Last Minute

I have a short chapter on this further on but for now, if you're going last minute or going to book and check-in on the day itself, and have researched some of the lowest prices, again, have a look at HotelTonight, Trivago (they search 250 sites alone, and several lesser-known sites, including Agoda, and also include sites like Expedia, Priceline, and Booking.com) Hotelscombined, there are others but I don't want to overload you, and these are solid and cover so many booking engines, so I'm going with them as they've never let me down. Then book in late in the evening, most of the rooms will have been taken if they're busy, and they'll know what their inventory is, and you'll get a good price and maybe even a free upgrade if you're pleasant to them at check-in.

## 28. Pay in the currency of the site

On the site that you're booking on, pay in the local currency of the site IF your card doesn't charge foreign transaction fees. If you want to book in your own currency and/or if your card charges foreign transaction fees, you can switch the currencies on Trivago, and Hotelscombined etc at the top of your screen. Switch the currency, and use xe.com to check if there's a significant difference.

## 29. The Hotel's Credit Card

If the hotel you want to stay at offers a credit card, you might look at taking it. Some cards will offer you free nights. MGM Resorts have one that you can apply for here (U.S. residents only).

https://www.mgmresorts.com/en/mlife-rewards-program/mlife-rewards-mastercard.html

## 30. Stay in someone's house!

House Sitting! I've touched on this, but it needs a little paragraph of its own. If you have time on your side as regards booking, and want to stay in Las Vegas for FREE, if you would like to look after someone's property and their animals, why don't you register with these guys?

www.trustedhousesitters.com This will be a runner for some of you for sure.

## 31. Buy Travel Insurance!

This is very important – as soon as you've booked your flights and/or hotel, buy Travel Insurance (especially if you're travelling to the U.S. from abroad). If you need to cancel, you'll want to get your hotel and flight money back. Honestly, you'll never know when you might need it, and trust me, I have a bit of experience of this, and hospitals and medical treatment in Nevada are NOT CHEAP.

## 32. FREE STAY! Half price rooms, reduced rooms, discounted show tickets, cheaper meals etc

Ok, finally, I kept you waiting for this, my apologies, but it'll be worth it (!), so here it is, myVegas and Wynn Slots. MyVegas first. Links are on my site. More opportunities to get FREE rooms, and lots of other discounted, BOGO (buy one, get one free) and FREE stuff. myVegas is the official mobile and Facebook game of MGM Resorts and M life Rewards. This is a free-to-play app that offers a plethora of slot and table games and gives you amazing rewards from MGM Resorts destinations.  You can earn free hotel rooms, meals, show tickets, and more.

The more you play, and the bigger you bet, the more "loyalty points" you earn. Open the App or the Facebook game every day and play, even for a minute or two at a time (but do open it each day as you get a free spin to give you points), and watch the loyalty points fly up. I know many people who use this App, I use it too, and the bonuses are worth playing for. It seems that you get the most loyalty points if you play it on Facebook. I read elsewhere that if you're on Android if you download myVegas from the Amazon App store, you get more loyalty points. I'm unsure as to why this is, but there you have it. I downloaded it from Google Play so I'm not really able to test this claim at the moment as you can only have one account. Most of the rewards are for the MGM resorts casinos in Las Vegas with some others for London etc. The rewards are DEFINITELY worth playing for. Make sure to read the small print of each reward as some will need to be used in short order once you take them. When you're in Las Vegas, you will go to an MGM casino (there are lots of them) to the "Mlife Players Club" desk, and sign up for their Mlife loyalty program. You give them your emailed confirmation there. The Mlife card will help you earn free slot credit as you spend in their casinos and also, your purchases there will gain you further points. Just to note: For a Mirage Mlife reward, you need to go to the Mirage Mlife Players Club to activate it, Bellagio reward, go to Bellagio to activate it, etc. It's very clear on the App once you read the screen, so you don't need me to go any further here.

WYNN SLOTS! Is this the best for last? Maybe, maybe not! You might curse me after this, or you might hug me. Depends on you, for sure. It will take you some time though. There's no denying this. With Wynn Slots, you can earn up to 4 nights free stays (while avoiding the universally hated RESORT FEES) in what is most certainly one of the most beautiful hotels in the world, and this is no exaggeration. They have won awards up to their eyeballs. AAA, 5 Diamond. With 19 in total,

Wynn Resorts have the most Forbes Travel Guide Five-Star Awards of Any Independent Hotel Company. If you have a partner, they can earn 4 nights too, so immediately, you have 8 free night's stay in what would be among many people's opinion as the best in Las Vegas. One of the very best in the World for sure. Maybe not for everyone but I don't think I'd ever say no. Go and see for yourself. Let me know though!

**A FINAL ONE ... can't leave this one out.**

While you're in Las Vegas, IF you have your own place at home, why don't you Airbnb it, to make yourself some money while you're away? Who knows, might even cover your Las Vegas hotel costs.

# CHAPTER 4 - BOOKING A LAS VEGAS HOTEL AT THE LAST MINUTE

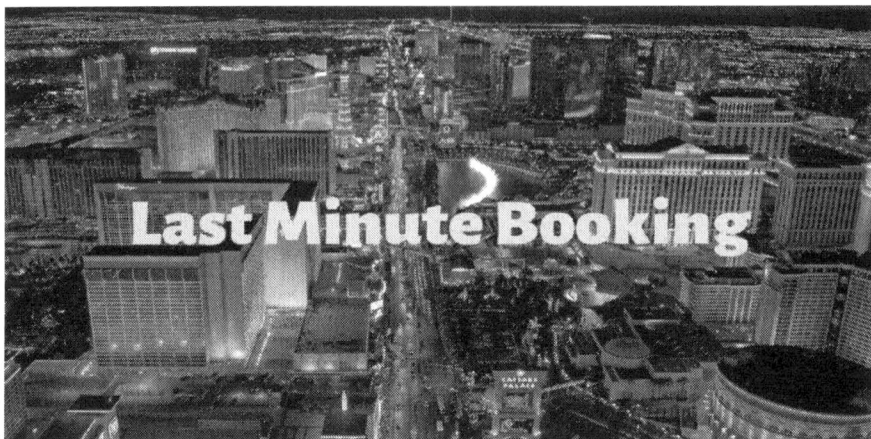

You're about to set off for Las Vegas, or you've arrived and you haven't got a hotel room yet. Panic stations! Deep breaths, I have you. You want to get the BEST POSSIBLE PRICE that you can. Sometimes leaving it late like this can have a small element of risk, but you're going to Las Vegas, so you're possibly someone that likes a little gamble, so if you can hold off, OR you were just booking late, I would HIGHLY recommend (and you can book on the day you arrive or a few days before), the "Hotel Tonight" app.

Hotel Tonight are given unsold rooms by hotels and they pass them onto you and I, at very often, super rates. Be aware though, I'd ask you always, if you are in any way unsure of the rate, to compare it with the same hotel on Trivago and the list of offers that I'm compiling for you on site. I can't see how you'd go wrong if you follow this, except, I wouldn't know if it would come up Trumps if you rock up into town on New Year's Eve (the busiest day of the year in Las Vegas and room prices are in the Stratosphere (not the hotel!) but the rest of the year, you should be fine. Some of the Hotel Tonight rates won't be the cheapest available, and that's why I'd always ask you to compare. I'm cautious enough by nature (good news for you!), certainly with spending hundreds or thousands, so before I book with anyone, those are the steps I'd take if I was in a hurry, and just didn't want to pay any more than was absolutely necessary.

You can book using Hotel Tonight a full 100 days in advance, and book a stay for as long as 14 days and a week in advance for stays of up to 5 nights. I have never been anything but fully delighted with this App and it's got me some sweet deals in the past. I'd love you to read to the end here though. It's important and I will save you further money.

I've booked hotels in all manner of ways in Las Vegas over the years, depending on the time of year, who I was staying with, all manner of factors. Don't get me wrong here, the hotels own sites, and the numerous sites that you might book on, ebookers, expedia, hotels.com, trivago, priceline, etc can all have fantastic deals and do have most of the time (I've used them all) but if I'm looking for something LAST MINUTE AND need to save money AND WANT TO KNOW That I'm in all probability getting the best deal possible, I'll always look to this app (Hotel Tonight) a few days before (comparing it with Trivago results) and again, you can compare it with the deals that I'm providing on the site. Between all of these, I'd be fairly sure that you can be happy that you've got a decent deal. I've also got €20 OFF your booking for you, or the equivalent in your money. Download the app on my site and then use this code sdonnelly18 (copy and paste it) you will GET €20 OFF your booking with them and I'll get €20 off a future booking of mine after you've booked, so thanks very much! You win, AND you help me too! We're like a right little mutual admiration society, aren't we?

Please ALSO note – Hotel Tonight bookings are NON-REFUNDABLE, so that's why I'd book it on the day itself (where possible) when I know that a flight interruption or what have you doesn't get in the way.

# CHAPTER 5 - AN EASY TO FOLLOW METHOD, TO GIVE YOURSELF THE BEST CHANCE OF GETTING A GREAT VALUE STAY DEAL

A quick yet wide search for a Las Vegas hotel

I'm going to show you how you might search for a hotel in Las Vegas, and be comfortable that you've got a very good price. This is the very least I'd do as regards finding the best price in the shortest time possible. I'll do a video at some point but for those that like to read, this should do the job.

TODAY is Wednesday, February 27th, 2019 and I'm going to do two searches here, both are for a 7-night stay. The first thing that you'd do before you search for prices is to have a quick look at the hotels in Las Vegas and their reviews so you can pick out some to zone in on.

I've done two searches, both for excellent hotels, and to note, at different times of the year, these hotels will be cheaper. The Bellagio search (the second one, is seven to eight months away from today, so right now won't be the cheapest time to book this, regardless, I did a search on it as many people will very happily book a hotel 7 to 8 months ahead of their visit. Me, I'll do it a few months prior normally or sometimes on the day itself with the HotelTonight App. If I were you, and if I have time on my side, I'd also be playing the Wynn Slots App and the MyVegas App with the possibility of getting some or all of the stay for free. Download them from the site, and then read on.

## The FIRST SEARCH – The Mirage

The first search, The Mirage, is 7 weeks away today, to be exact, it's April 17th to 24th 2019 (7 nights, double room) and again, the Bellagio one is for October 2nd to October 9th 2019. Also, the Mirage booking is a busy time (as is October for the Bellagio) so this isn't a terrible price.

I decided to look at the prices for The Mirage. The Mirage is a beautiful 4-star hotel casino on the Strip that you can't really go wrong staying in.

I started by looking on the Mirage site itself first.

Then I'd always check Trivago (these guys search north of 250 sites, including sites like Expedia, Priceline, and Booking.com).

I'd always check Hotelscombined too (another great aggregator site like Trivago).

I checked the HotelTonight App also but they weren't selling rooms at the Mirage, unfortunately.

**NOTE:** On both this search and search 2 (Bellagio) I have also checked the Google Hotel Prices. They weren't in the running price-wise so I've omitted them to keep this piece as short and as uncomplicated as possible.

You'll suddenly find that you're doing three comparisons but in truth, you're doing so much more than that as Trivago and Hotelscombined are aggregator sites, which means that they'll be checking hundreds of others including hotels.com, booking.com, expedia, roomdi, travelup, anoma, ebookers, travelrepublic, agoda, otel, amongst so many more so it'll be difficult to beat this search.

DATES: April 17th to April 24th 2019 (7 nights)

ROOM TYPE: Resort King

HERE are the results in order (ALL include taxes and resort fees – BE VERY CAREFUL to check that these are included PRIOR to any booking):

Mirage.com comes in at $1,249.45

On Trivago (aggregator site), the site TravelUp (great reviews on TrustPilot of 8.8/10 with 54,663 reviews as of today, February 27th, 2019, so we're cool) was $958.55

On HotelsCombined (aggregator site), the site Otel.Com was $1,186.27

**FINDINGS HERE...** Trivago won by providing us the TravelUp price as it had the best deal $958.55 and came in $290.90 cheaper than Mirage.Com and $227.72 cheaper than the second-best price which was the Otel.Com one of $1,186.27.

## The SECOND SEARCH -The Bellagio

The second search, I went to look for prices for The Bellagio. I'm not going to mention anything about the Bellagio here, as I think most know that The Bellagio is a Top-Notch 5-star hotel casino in the centre of the Strip.

I continued with my process and looked in this order.

Bellagio own site first, Bellagio.Com

Then Trivago

Then Hotelscombined

Due to this being more than 100 days away I was unable to check HotelTonight for these dates.

As with the first search, I also checked Google Hotels on this one but they couldn't compete on this price-wise either.

DATES: October 2nd to October 9th 2019 (7 nights)

ROOM TYPE: Resort Tower King

HERE are the results in order (ALL include taxes and resort fees – BE VERY CAREFUL to check that these are included PRIOR to any booking):

Bellagio.com comes in at $2,518.17

On Trivago (aggregator site), the site TravelUp (again great reviews on TrustPilot of 8.8/10 with 54,663 reviews as of today, February 27th, 2019, so we're cool) was $1,922.78

On HotelsCombined (aggregator site), the site Agoda was cheapest on their platform at $2193.69 and included two buffets but still more expensive than TravelUp provided by Trivago.

**FINDINGS HERE...** Trivago won again with TravelUp at $1,922.78 being a HUGE $595.39 cheaper than Bellagio.com AND being $270.91 cheaper than Agoda (although Agoda did have 2 FREE Buffets, it was still more expensive in the long run)

## WHAT TO TAKE FROM THESE TWO SEARCHES?

These were quite simple searches (with these two hotels just chosen as examples, you can do this with any Las Vegas hotels) I go more in-depth with searching but I wanted to show you a quick simple method (if you have a firm idea of the hotel that you want) that will cover as many sites as quickly as possible by including two massive aggregator sites (Trivago and Hotelscombined) and the comparison to the hotels own site. Now, also to note, the hotels own sites in these examples, Mirage and Bellagio will match prices found on other sites so you could, and if you have a players card for the hotel casino in question (or will get one when you get there), you could call them and get them to match the price and thus hopefully get rewarded in the future. The worst that can happen is that they say no. They will probably say yes though, as they get their money immediately and don't have to wait to receive it from another site, like TravelUp, Otel or Agoda in these examples. Up to you of course. Just a few tips. Also, to note, in case it looks like the aggregator sites will always be cheaper than the hotels own sites, this isn't solid fact, as the hotels own site can be cheaper, just not in these examples.

**YOU NEED TO CHECK A FEW SITES**, is the motto here AND ensure that you factor in the taxes and resort fees IF the site hasn't made this clear. IF they haven't, YOU can get a nasty surprise upon checking out.

# CHAPTER 6 - TIPS FOR GETTING THE BEST VALUE FLIGHTS TO LAS VEGAS AND "PRETTY SOLID" ADVICE ON HOW YOU CAN AVOID KILLING YOUR CAT.

## Don't be overly-choosey with your airline choice unless...

They aren't providing things that you'd 100% expect, or if they're adding on extras that you wouldn't consider right. Otherwise, they're just getting you from A to B, some a little bit fancier than others but in the main, your bum/butt will be comfy regardless of your airline, unless you have piles (haemorrhoids), and if you do, I've no experience with this to help you out. You've picked up the wrong book, but listen, the seat might still be fine even if you do have piles. I have sympathy with you if you have them though. From hearing before, these can help, Retinol (OTC cream) and the use of a "ring cushion". Who is naming these things? My God. I didn't expect this airline choice segment to turn out like this, my fault because I probably shouldn't have mentioned piles. I know nothing about them, nor am I a Doctor of Medicine (I can put you in touch with the Good Doctor though. Not the TV show dude. This "Good Doctor", he's a pal of mine, and loves that title) so you'll need to consult your own, sorry about this. Woah, glad that's that one over. That was kinda stressful. Ok, onwards and upwards!

## Don't always fly direct...

You can often save money by going from a different airport. There was this situation where I was going with a best buddy of mine a few years back. He was living in Wales and I was in Dublin. I'd found flights that were Dublin, London Gatwick, Las Vegas. Aer Lingus from Dublin to London Gatwick and Virgin Atlantic from London Gatwick to Las Vegas. Return flights, one connection going out and one coming back, same airport each time, London Gatwick. I'd gone that route before so I was happy to get that ticket and needed to see what Richie thought, what with him being in Wales. My idea in my head, was that he'd only need to get himself to London (being on the landmass of the UK) and take the Virgin Atlantic flight straight to Las Vegas, the same one as me and that he'd get it cheaper as he wouldn't be doing the Dublin – London or the return London – Dublin parts of the flight. That was then the plan. I'd meet Richie in Gatwick and we'd jump on the flight and next stop Las Vegas, but as with all stories like this, there's a road bump. The road bump was, for Richie to get that flight, and then we'd be on the same flight, there and back, it was going to cost him £200 (UK pounds) more than my ticket and mine had extra journeys! Remember I was going from Dublin to London and then on the way back, it was London to Dublin. So, Richie ended up buying the same tickets as me and got a Ryanair flight over from Cardiff to meet me at Dublin airport and we went from there. So, the moral of the story here is, look at any airports near you, even if it means getting a short flight there IF it's worth it to you. That holiday, maybe the greatest so far (I think is a fair comment), as lovely little Richie's have resulted from that trip. What there is to be learnt from this also, is that often it's cheaper to fly from another airport (even in a different country) than it is to fly from your own, EVEN if it's got a part of the same journey from your local airport. Strange eh? Yet very true. Fingers crossed that this doesn't lead to a massive influx of UK holidaymakers taking the cheaper flights from Ireland and putting the prices up on me!

## Early morning and late-night flights are cheaper...

That's just the way things are.

## Be flexible with your route as regards connecting flights...

If it takes an extra hour but saves you $40 or so on the flight, is it worth it to you? This will depend on your salary I suppose, but to many people, taking an extra hour getting to where they're going an hour later, and to save $40, yeah that's going to be cool. It's always best though if that extra time is spent in the air, as when you're on the ground in the airport, waiting on a connecting flight, there are going to be so many distractions waiting for your money. Food, drinks, and then there are the shops. Best to be waiting on flights in between for as little time possible in this regard, but of course, not with such a short connection as to put you in danger of missing your flight. I'm not that keen on a connection time of fewer than two hours or so, as often the first flight can be delayed, plus if this happens and you're connecting in an airport like Heathrow in London, with buses to catch and at times up to three securities to go through, it's really out of your control pretty much, and can be an anxious time wondering if you'll make your flight, especially with the queues there.

## Fly during the week...

It's cheaper than the weekend PLUS hotels are cheaper during the week in Las Vegas too, much cheaper!

## Fly when others aren't...

Late Autumn and Winter in Las Vegas are normally times that you'll get very good flight deals to Las Vegas. They're also times that you'll get great hotel rates (except New Year's Eve obviously, when you'll be absolutely robbed). Also, I've often seen great prices for flights to and from Las Vegas in July and August but obviously you'll need to be very wary of the heat at that time of the year.

## Search for your flights using SkyScanner.Net or Momondo...

These are flight search aggregator sites that will help you find the cheapest, quickest, best, and fastest flights. Prices can differ a little, and in either sites favour at times, so there's no outright winner here for me although I'll admit that I'm more familiar with SkyScanner as I've been using that more often.

**Search SkyScanner by "cheapest month" ...**

With this trick you get to see all the flight prices for each day of the month and you can look at as many months as you like. You simply go to the site, I'd choose from Dublin to Las Vegas, you pick your own city obviously. Then where it asks for the date, you simply choose "whole month" and then "cheapest month". There you go, enjoy! That's definitely going to save you money

**You should use the tracking facility in Skyscanner...**

To get them to email you price increases/decreases for certain dates that you'd like to go. It's quite exciting getting the emails with the rises and falls. Definitely a nice way to keep an eye on your flight dates without booking them straight away.

**There's an app called Hopper...**

(I had a cat with the same name. She had only three working legs, thus her name, well her name was originally Hudson but we called her Ace and called Ace, Hudson, so Ace was then Hopper (you love me confusing you don't you?) so depending on who you spoke to, there'd be confusion, but not if Hopper was mentioned (as she only had three working legs). There were three of them and their mum, they were all named after alcohol, but that's nothing to do with flights, and yeah, alcohol, that explains a lot of things. Anyway, their names were Buzz, Ace, Rocky and Hudson. There you go now, cats, alcohol (don't give cats booze, don't) and flying for you. Here's an important thing about cats though, NEVER EVER give them Aspirin. They will die from internal bleeding. Something my Grandfather didn't know and we lost a beauty called Tom due to this). Anyway, back to "technology Hopper". They'll show you analysis and track your flight dates for you also. This is a handy one to look at.

## When you get the price that you're happy with...

From whichever site it happens to be, always check the flight price against the site of the airline itself. If it's not the same on the airline's site, see if they'll price match it for you as it's more beneficial for you to book with the airline rather than a third party. Most of the time and I've used third parties maybe half the time, and they're fine, but ensure that you're choosing brands that you know of (Expedia, ebookers, Orbitz, whichever), but if something goes wrong, it's best if you'd booked directly with the airline, whether that's online or by phone is up to you. If there's a delay, cancellation, or if you need to make a change to the booking (third parties often charge for this and some airlines do too), for any of these reasons you're best having booked directly. You'll also be able to collect frequent flyer miles.

# CHAPTER 7 - 6 AFFORDABLE AND TASTY PLACES, THAT I'D DEFINITELY RECOMMEND FOR YOU TO EAT AND DRINK IN

## FRENCH - MON AMI GABI

Beautiful French Food, People Watching, Bellagio Water Show, Romance at Mon Ami Gabi

Suggestion - Ham and Cheese Crepe at Mon Ami Gabi, Paris Las Vegas

Ok, this is going to be so so easy to write for many reasons, but they'll hold for another day. I have memories of here that will stay with me forever. Mon Ami Gabi is a wonderful restaurant, and with the memories I have of there, it's as close to perfect as

perfect can be for me. It's not expensive but nor is it cheap. It's excellent value for what it provides, and it provides on different levels. Mon Ami Gabi is top quality AND obviously part of my aim with the site is to help you to experience Las Vegas luxury too, for what I believe to be good value. I'm covering two options for you here, both great value, one being cheaper than the other, so this will help you with your decision. For me it's no decision. Mon Ami is nailed on in many of my Las Vegas thoughts. Mon Ami Gabi or just Mon Ami, as I've heard many locals call it. You really should visit here, like, definitely! I'm not trying to sell this. I haven't been paid anything, and being honest, if people start going there based on this, well that's very cool, but don't deny me a seat! You'll have a great memory. Bring me too! This is one of the very first places I'll visit each time I go to Las Vegas and one of the last when I'm leaving. I've been many times now. Mon Ami Gabi is, from recollection, one of the five highest-grossing restaurants in America. I'm weird. I'm interested in stuff like that. I like to see what makes the best, the best. I'm not surprised that it's placed that highly though, as it's absolutely excellent in every way. It's a favourite Brunch spot for many locals. Get a seat on the patio (that's first come/first served) for THE BEST people watching on the Strip, some of the best food that many people will ever taste in their lives, AND the perfect position to watch and listen to the Bellagio Water Show.

If you want to eat at Mon Ami Gabi, for the best possible value (and this is one of the aims of my book obviously), and fill your tummy up, then go for lunch, and have the crepe with ham and cheese AND mash (you'll need to ask them to substitute the French Fries for this BUT do it! Trust me!) or go for the croque monsieur, again, have it with mash. Make sure to have the mash! Both are incredibly good options with mash – filling! I'm from Ireland… I just know a few things about spuds. I have a book, soon to be a major Hollywood film, called "I know what you did last summer with that potato". Andddd we're back. Just to clarify, I don't have a major Hollywood movie in the works, at least not about any potatoes that I'm aware of. Back to the food, each of these will cost you under $15 from memory AND you really won't mind paying that I would think. When you taste it, you'll really won't mind! I think so anyway. I'd have paid far more for this wonderful food, with the location, sitting practically on the Strip, the staff are always wonderful, and the entire experience of Mon Ami Gabi. I think I've probably eaten here well over a dozen times now (four- or five-times last trip) and it never disappoints. It's consistently outstanding, and if you want a place to be consistently anything, outstanding is it. Again… trust me, do this! This is NOT to be missed, especially if you have a special someone to share it with. If you've a few more dollars to spare, do have a special night here by eating out on the patio. Here's the suggestion if so… Onion

Soup Au Gratin (this is really great, and to compare, I've had it in Paris, France, numerous times and Dublin obviously. Not boasting, Paris is very close to Dublin), a Prime Steak Frites (Prime Steak), choose your sauce, and again, have it with mash instead of chips, TRUST me on the sunscreen, I mean the mash, but wear sunscreen and get to know your parents, you never know when they'll be gone for good. For Dessert, Vanilla Bean Creme Brulee (c'est magnifique). This will come to around $53 per person. Any taxes, tips on top. Is it worth it? 100%, every time, EVERY single time. A night you won't easily forget. Can't wait to go again myself now!

DO NOT NOT go here. This means, GO HERE! You'll love it. Do your best to get a patio seat (they are a first come, first served) for the best experience. I could go on about Mon Ami Gabi for hours but I have to give the others a fair shot too. Mon Ami Gabi, you've given me what I will hold forever in my thoughts amongst the most beautiful moments in life. Thank you. All going well, I'll see you again very soon.

## THAI - LE THAI DOWNTOWN LAS VEGAS

Suggestion - Drunken Noodles (Pad Kee Mow) at Le Thai, Downtown

This is YUMMY! It's Downtown at 523 Fremont Street and it's called "Le Thai".

Right... what you should have here, AND it's not expensive. IF you go for lunch you can get the lunch special, where you'd choose from almost any curry there, and you add your meat preference, or Tofu or Shrimp, for ONLY $9.95, and they give you a soft drink (Coke, Iced Tea, Lemonade etc) with it. This is a really nice deal and it'll be delicious. I'd like to recommend another dish too, a little more expensive, but still very good value. I had the "Drunken Noodles". Mother of God almighty, you'd actually sell your mother for these, but don't, that's not going to work out well for anyone, and I think that it's illegal anyway, so no selling mothers, even mother-in-laws, the same laws apply (I think). Back to the food, Pad Kee Mow is the real name for these. Look, I'm not going to go into big detail, as it's been a little while and I can't remember it exactly but I do remember that it was just delicious and I want it again! I'm just telling you, go for this, if you don't, you don't.

In fact, you could probably go for anything on the menu (many friends kept telling me about this gem of a place, but I had to visit it myself) and I'm going back for more of it as soon as time allows. Another day (I really like the food here!) I had the Tom Kha soup with Shrimp ($12 I think) ... it was HUGE! The Tom Kha is a coconut soup with chicken, mushroom, lemongrass, lemon juice and with green onion and cilantro (in Europe we call this Coriander, also known as Chinese Parsley). Again, holy Mother of God... if you have a few bob, get both the soup and the dinner if there are two of you and you can share them. This is some of THE BEST hangover type food you could eat, plus the spicy food helps you burn calories quicker, and you'll need to do this with all your partying in Las Vegas.

Oh yeah, of course (!), I haven't forgotten, there is another very good Thai restaurant, it's called Lotus of Siam. It's off the Strip and is a locals favourite also. I was lucky enough to eat here also, and another day, I'll tell you about it. I'm going to need another visit to Lotus though as it was a while ago. You'll need to get an Uber or a Lyft to it. Definitely worth a visit though if you're cool with going "off-strip". In related news... Lotus of Siam have opened at a second location, so clearly, business is good!

You won't go wrong with either of these restaurants. Definitely not.

## BURGERS AND MORE - STRIPBURGER AND CHICKEN!

All right

I got something to say

Yeah, it's better to burn out

Yeah, than fade away

That's the magnificent Def Leppard there above with Rock of Ages from the multi-platinum selling album Hysteria from 1987. Sorry, I'm not a DJ, and this is a site about Las Vegas, but I love this band since I was 14, and the third line seems apt, "I got something to say", so I thought that I'd sing you the introduction.

See, I'm even singing for you here. How many books will offer that service? You can't sue me for this...

It was December 10th 2010, no it wasn't cold, and it was night number one in Las Vegas for my Dad. I was meant to go over for the 11 days with a friend but they had to cancel. I was happy to go on my own of course (as I enjoy that too) but my Mum thought that it might do my Dad good to go, as he'd had a stroke a little prior and needed a holiday. Being honest I knew that he didn't really want to go, so I didn't press him on it and what would happen would happen, but it turned out that whether he wanted to go or not, he'd be going. Like in many families, he might not be the boss, but don't tell him that. Turned out that my Mum was right to take no prisoners as he loved it!

Right, anyway, back to the night. We'd arrived in Las Vegas and I'd found us a great deal at the Wynn beforehand. From memory, as some of you might want to know, I got the return flights (Dublin to London Gatwick – Aer Lingus) and London Gatwick to Las Vegas (Virgin Atlantic) AND 10 nights at the magnificently beautiful Wynn for in and around €900 each. That's a very good deal as the flights themselves are normally averaging around the €500 mark from Ireland (you can get cheaper at times but also, far more expensive options too) and if you've ever seen or stayed at the Wynn I think you'll agree with that as regards it being a very nice deal. Anyway, this post isn't about the flight or the Wynn. After checking into the hotel (we got an upgrade and no resort fee which was very cool…. I'll tell you how again, it wasn't difficult), getting showered and changed, it was time for a pint! We're Irish and its always time for a pint, isn't it? Well I don't drink these days but before then, yeah, it was hard to find a time that, for almost any occasion in Ireland, you might be expected to drink. Walked out of the Wynn and straight across the road to Stripburger being totally unaware of how, in the years to follow, that this lovely place and the people there, would come to play a very real part in my life. People think, ah it's Vegas, it's not real. It is real I can assure you! We were greeted at the entrance and sat at the bar. Straight away, a lovely lady behind the bar, she introduced herself. Her name was Amy, she was the bartender, and Amy came to be a great friend of mine. Amy is a true superstar of the Strip. A top TOP quality person and I'm very proud and always so happy, to have her as a friend of mine. She makes the famous "Amy's Strong Island Iced Tea". Stripburger is renowned for it.

We started on our pints, had some more and then got some food. To not use the Lord's name here, the food was Deelish! We had sliders cooked perfectly, so juicy I can still nearly smell them, really gorgeous sauce on the buns, I'm getting really hungry now recalling this and I've no access to Stripburger today damnit. We had atomic fries…. can't explain this right now as I'm getting overwhelmed just thinking about how high they were piled and the spice craziness that went on in my mouth… so good! Last but not least of the food, and something that has lived with me to this day (I didn't bring them home on the plane and preserve them, just to be clear), I mean that taste…. and we don't have these in Ireland (well I haven't found them yet anyway), fried pickles with ranch sauce. Good God it was a bit of heaven for me. This was my virgin fried pickle and what a bar to lose that virginity in! If you are going to Las Vegas…. EAT these things! You can worry about losing the weight later, or just do lots of walking around in Vegas. I'm telling you here and now. These are the business! Plus…. finish them off with a Butterscotch, Banana and Rum Milkshake. Definitely! Don't miss that! Here, this is actually good fun, telling you about these foods and I'm reliving great memories as I am. Anyway, that's just some of the food. The turkey burger is a real beaut too, really juicy!

In 2011, I had my jaw broken in Las Vegas on the first night of a two week stay, by a stranger in an unprovoked attack (again… for another day… I'll actually give you rules, which if you follow them, can help you avoid getting your jaw broken in any city hopefully), anyhoo, at this time, Amy and Mark there, they both helped me so much as regards getting food into me. There was NOTHING that they wouldn't have liquidized for me. I had my mouth wired shut, I mean my teeth were locked down on top of each other, and I could only take liquids through a straw. Some of the best people, Amy and Mark, and God I needed them at that time. Mark came to be a great friend of mine also. He's an ace, a really great guy, and I know that all his staff would easily testify to that too. Miss you Brotha! Anyway... I'm getting away from the evening there. My Dad and I ended up drinking a fair bit of Tequila along with a number of beers, and well it's hard to remember the rest of the night! Oh yeah.... I remember! I ended up in Blush back in the Wynn. No, not in a hedge, in Blush. It was a boutique (that's the name for this type of club apparently) nightclub inside the Wynn that was recommended to me by the ladies running the reception on the Tower Suites (see I told you we got upgraded, Tower Suites, woohoo!), who, get this...sent me around with the manager's name (he was their former boss from what I understood), and they told me to avoid the queue entirely and just go up and ask for him by name. That was very cool of them! Anyway, again.... another story for another day, and we are friends to this very day too. What a crazy night that turned out to be... in the long term I mean, as regards making new friends. Three great people in the one night, lottery stuff! They're the best nights too, the nights you make new friends. Oh and on that, when we first sat down at Stripburger that night, after saying hi to Amy, telling her about why we were there, like most

I suppose, on holiday (vacation), Amy made it her business to introduce us to everyone in the bar! Now if that's not the best bartending you'll ever see, I can't tell you what is. You can't help but make new friends at this bar!

Listen to me.... GO THERE. You won't regret it. You might be unlucky enough to meet me there! It's the first and last bar I'll go to on each trip. You'll be sitting out in the open air, eating the most beautiful food, being served by the wonderful, and fun staff, possibly making new life-long friends and having the nicest drinks...oh yeah and ask for Amy's "Strong Island Iced Tea" ... You'll love it but listen to Amy when you get it.... two is enough for anyone and maybe too much for some. Trust a previous passer-outer on this. I'm not saying how many I had (more than two, I'm tall) or how many other drinks I had beforehand of course! I'm Irish and by God I could drink, but too many of these and it will knock the head off you! And that's if Amy doesn't have it laughed off you beforehand! Go go go! Don't hesitate! I bloody love you Stripburger! (and Chicken!)

Fashion Show Mall (Across from the Wynn) 3200 Las Vegas Boulevard South

Las Vegas, NV, 89109

(702) 737-8747

Sun – Thurs: 11:00 AM – 12:00 AM

Fri – Sat: 11:00 AM – 1:00 AM

Happy Hour: 4-7 PM & 10 PM – Close

## PUB AND CAFE - The Village Pub and Cafe

There is a great Steak Deal at Ellis Island Las Vegas...

Well so, is it the cheapest steak in Las Vegas? It's the cheapest that I've found (if you find one cheaper let me know, but at this price, I don't think we're going to argue over a couple of dollars) and it's very good for the price! PLUS, it comes with soup or salad!

I lived just a couple of minutes' walk from this place at the Meridian on Koval and East Flamingo, only yards away from where Tupac had his life taken, and it was the first place I ever had food in Las Vegas. That was in December 2008, my first night in Las Vegas, staying at Paris, went for a walk with friends, we got a little lost (but not really as it's only a few minutes' walk from the Strip) and ended up here. I kept going back because if you're looking for a good value feed of any type, but definitely of a low-priced steak, then this is the one for you.

Ellis Island is on Koval Lane and it's just behind Paris and Bally's so that you can get your bearings. It's a hotel, casino and micro-brewery and get this, EVERY day that there's football on (American football) the 20-ounce Ellis Island craft beers are only $1! On Sunday this can be the majority of the day. Can you get buzzed cheaper in Las Vegas? Yeah but probably only if you're getting it for free. I used to drink their IPA, it was tasty! I never really drank for the taste, just for the buzz, as most drinks with booze didn't really do it for me but I did love their IPA. The craft beers of theirs, they are an absolute steal at $2.25 the rest of the time I believe AND ALSO, it's ONLY $5 for wings, sliders or a hot dog and fries during the NFL games. Very hard to beat, and the dollar beers are also on offer for the Las Vegas Golden Knights Ice Hockey games, who play nearly every second night. I believe this price starts two hours before the game…. BUT back to the steak…. $7.99 TOP SIRLOIN STEAK SPECIAL!!! Available all day, every day! 10 oz, Filet-Cut, Top Sirloin Steak, served with your choice of potato or rice, garlic green beans and home-made soup or salad. I get it with the baked potato and normally soup (depending on which one is on that day). Melt a nice bit of butter on the spud (it's a HUGE potato!), season it with salt and pepper and then pile on the sour cream… SO SO GOOD! I'm a big spud fan if you didn't know already… well I am from Ireland, so OBVS! To get the deal though…. Please read to the end as you'll need a Players card and that's easy to get. It'll only take a few minutes out of your day.

Now, the first time there, it was very troublesome for me to understand the poor waiter's accent, and apparently for him, mine, from the carry on that we had. "Super Salad" is what I heard. "yeah, what's that?" I said never having heard of a super salad before. I thought it might just be an enormous salad with extra surprises. He repeated himself then and you could tell that he was tired. "Yeah, Super Salad, what is that?" I said. At this point, the people with me (my ex-work colleagues) were laughing. I wasn't getting it, not at all and had no idea what they were laughing at but that wasn't bothering me. It was past 3 am, this was probably too much for the poor guy and yeah for me, my brain had long gone to sleep. "No sir, it's a choice, soup or salad" he said. "aha!" I said. "I'm sorry, I'd no idea. I got confused. What's the soup? I think I'll have soup". Anyway, the next table over got flipped up and over at the exact same time by a lady who was clearly very angry with the guy she was sitting beside. Everything went up in the air. A huge lone potato made its way onto the floor close by and it stayed there for the duration of our meal. Now, this isn't to put Ellis Island down because I love the place, it's just, well, there's probably no need to mention the potato but I have now so I'll just leave it there, like it was at that moment. I don't believe that the waiter saw it, and he'd probably just about had enough, what with me not understanding his clear (for him) English and the tip from the upturned table possibly not making its way into his pocket that evening. Anyway...back to the steak.... you should go for this. For sure you should! Have it in the Karaoke bar, I think that's the only place you can have it bar (pardon the pun) the restaurant. The bar in the centre of the casino (it's a small casino), I'm not so sure that they serve food at that, I've only drank at that bar a couple of times but the Karaoke one, dozens of times and it's comfier too.

LASTLY on the steak... well on the soup that comes with it.... GO ON A FRIDAY for the most delicious White Clam Chowder soup. Well I'd never had Clam Chowder soup anywhere else before so I can't compare it with anywhere BUT I can tell you this, it's bloody beautiful, wonderfully creamy AND the locals keep coming back for it, so that's probably the best sign that you need.

The staff are really nice. I had the pleasure of being served by Shannon and Eugene at different times. Really nice people! There's a lovely English lady working there for years too and she has put the football (soccer) on for me when I needed it. I just can't remember her name at this moment. Rosie, I think. I'm the very worst with names. Her voice is unforgettable though, a heavy accent. I think Leeds in England. Honestly though, I've a terrible memory these days. Seriously good fun though and I've never seen her in bad form.

Finally, ... To get this steak deal ...YOU DO NEED to sign up for a players card in the casino (it's FREE) to get this for $7.99. To be totally accurate... the soup or salad and steak deal is $9.99 with the players card (still a total bargain) and if you gamble a fiver, you'll get it for $7.99. We're not going to argue over $2, are we? Also ... if you're keen on desserts, there's a decent cheesecake IF you can fit more in. That's nice but not exceptional, and no more than a fiver.

Stay after the game for karaoke or singing blackjack dealers. There's a really good Elvis there. Gary is his name. I think he performs on a Friday and Saturday at 5pm and he is definitely worth seeing. There's a Shakira impersonator too.

## MEXICAN - Mexican Munchie Nirvana at El Segundo Sol

El Segundo Sol, is a beautiful and superb Mexican Restaurant up at the Fashion Show Mall opposite the Wynn and Palazzo. It's beside Stripburger and Chicken, which I've written about for you also.

Now this is AMAZING FOOD! I say go here at any time! Except when it's closed. You won't get food when it's closed so I'm not sure how that might work out for you. I love El Segundo Sol. They have the potential to charge a fortune due to the quality of the food, the location, the service, but they don't, and I've got great respect for this. El Segundo offers good value for super quality PLUS if you go at Happy Hour time, well you're really kinda robbing these people, unfortunately.

Suggestion - All-Natural Chicken Fajitas

The super-uber-duperdy-duper-fantastico All-Natural Chicken fajitas I had there. Oh Mother of all that is good and holy. I've had them a few times now. They are now one of my favourite interplanetary dishes. High praise! They were on one of those sizzling plates with everything I needed. I think that there were six little bowls put with it. Sour cream. Black beans. Guacamole (their Guacamole is incredible! SO GOOOOOOOOODDDDDDDDD!). There was Pico de Gallo (deelish). A beautiful salsa, and the warmest tortillas wraps to put everything into. AND the rice ... the rice! WOW! That was epic! A beautiful coriander and garlic flavour. Honestly, I love this. I think it was about $19.99. Worth every cent. There was so much in it. Griddled bell peppers, onions, corn on the cob and asparagus. Top TOP stuff!

P.S. This is IMPORTANTE. This is HOW TO EAT DELICIOUS MEXICAN FOOD FOR VERY LITTLE MONEY...

"Loco Hour" (that's Happy Hour in English) is run daily from 4:00pm–7:00pm (the same as Stripburger and Chicken, next door) AND for $3 you can consume Two-Bite Tacos, $5 wonderful Quesadillas, $5 Margaritas (insanely gorgeous! IF you drink alcohol, these are NOT to be missed) and $3 Tequila shots and more. Just go, trust me. Go go go! Super food, wonderful staff, all tops in my book! If you fancy a drink afterwards, go next door to Stripburger and Chicken. They're a sister restaurant/bar and written about in this chapter. Try Amy's "Strong Island Ice T", that's drinking for you! Tell her that I sent you (I'd appreciate that and they'll hopefully still let you in!), and a big hello to everyone in both places from me, not that they all know me, a few of them will do though.

I highly recommend going here, especially if you're a fan of Mexican food. Really top stuff!

## DINER - Peppermill and Fireside Lounge

Ok, this is a MUST-VISIT for many reasons. Historical Las Vegas, romance (if you're with a partner or a possible one) and the obvious, food.

If you're out late in Las Vegas or on your way back to your hotel, absolutely starving after a night out. You're staying on the Strip (or not necessarily) and looking for somewhere to eat, have I got the place for you. Historic Las Vegas certainly. A very comfy place with HUGE portions of food! Even though there are tons of 24-hour eateries in Las Vegas, none have stood the test of time like Peppermill restaurant and Fireside lounge (they are two different rooms with the same main door entrance). It's very close to Encore (walking North towards The Stratosphere) and on that side of the Strip. Listen, this is a place that you really should check out and I know that I'm repeating myself here, it's just one not to miss! A locals favourite for sure. I reckon go into the Fireside lounge first, sit by the open fire pit (this is, just sort of too nice, it's a trap! No, it's not. If you have a partner with you, they are going to love it!) and have a cocktail (they are numerous and they are super). It's like maybe travelling in time and the Fireplace kinda reminds me of the Hot Tub Time-Machine film for some reason. I'll work that out yet.

Suggestion - Fresh Fruit with Banana Bread and Marshmallow Sauce.

I was first introduced to Peppermill by two friends that I'll never forget, Las Vegas locals (well, many years in Las Vegas, enough certainly to be called a local). My first time there was sitting beside the open Fireplace/pit that they have there in the lounge. Utter luxury without the cost of utter luxury, and you could really believe that you're in the 70s! I have the best memories of Peppermill for sure. It opened in 1972 (it's 50th isn't far off!) and is one of only a few buildings from that time on the Strip to still be there, and that's a great thing in a city that's always changing. It's also been the backdrop to films like "Casino" and "Showgirls", so you'll be tripling up by visiting here, with history, romance and gastronomia! I really love it here (I think you know this by now!), so comfy (not just because I'm getting old, this place is romantic to the extreme, and apparently it was voted as one of "America's 10 Best

Make-Out Bars" and if you get to the Fireplace/pit you'll understand! I don't think that it's very difficult to get these seats but they won't be for everyone. Turn left after coming in the main door or you'll miss it!).

Peppermill has beautiful drinks and good food. A great menu too. I think you'd find it very difficult not to find something for everyone here. I've had a SPECTACULAR "fresh fruit" dish. The size of it, it's massive! It comes with a full loaf of fresh banana-nut bread and a gorgeous creamy marshmallow sauce. The smell of banana from the freshly baked bread was incredible! This is one to get, if not for the bread alone, the spectacle of the fruit display itself, WOW! It's HUGE! I think I already said that!

As regards savoury food, I remember having the Lorraine Omelette, and this was yum! It was HUGE too and this isn't just because I'm European. I think the girl that served me said that there are 8 eggs in it. 8 eggs people, and the rest of what's in it, plus what it comes with! This will do you as regards your food intake for an entire day! I can never finish it and end up bringing half of it home with me (not to Ireland obvs, but to where-ever home is in Las Vegas at that time). It was made with, well obviously the eight eggs and then, diced bacon, sautéed green onions and melted Swiss cheese. It came with hash browns (yummy!!!) and then you have a choice of toast, English muffin, piping hot blueberry or lemon-cranberry muffin, or toasted bagel with cream cheese. So filling!

This isn't the cheapest eatery in Las Vegas, but it is NOT expensive for the portions that you get, and clearly not as I'm getting enough to bring home to have for lunch the next day! Obviously you get the whole historic experience of the place but, and I'll say this without reservation, that amount of food alone, the omelette and hash browns and whatever you choose with it really will fill you for many hours if not for an entire day, so $14.95 for it is money well spent for good food. Plus if you're coming here after clubbing in XS, Tryst or Surrender (all at Wynn Encore), the Peppermill is almost beside Encore, and if you can afford $15 a pop for a beer or what have you, this is far better value AND better for you! Your head will definitely thank you in the morning after the booze.

That MONSTER "fresh fruit" I mentioned will set you back $18.95. Is that worth it? You wouldn't buy it for one person, definitely not, but I think if there are 2 or more of you, sharing that for $9.48 each (two people), yep, for sure. Why not! The look of the thing itself is worthy of many photos! I don't think that's just me being Irish (we don't get food in huge portions like this in Europe), I just think it was utterly spectacular, and that's that. Definitely one for Instagram if you're on that. I am, but I've no idea how it works yet. I'll sort that.

As regards booze, you can buy a bottle of J. ROGET (sparkling wine) for $18, so if you want to get sauced, it's not as cheap as Walmart for sure, but you won't be going on a date to Walmart I imagine (or maybe you are, you're inventive if you are, but I don't know if your date will enjoy it, maybe!), and you'll be well on the way for a lot less than buying the fizz in nightclubs. I'm out of the drinking game right now but this is good value in a restaurant for a buzz.

Go to Peppermill, and don't forget to bring a date, you'll knock their socks off! DEFINITELY a place to visit! Put it on your list, I certainly would, and can't wait to go back again!

Suggestion - Crab Cakes! (I know it's the Desert...)

Another time I had the crab cakes... (there were three) ... GORGEOUS!!! With roasted red pepper cream sauce. I'm going back!

# FREE BONUS GUIDE

## ALMOST 100 PLACES WITH GREAT DEALS FOR GRUB AND THE DEMON IN LAS VEGAS

The following "almost 100" list of Bars and Restaurants and Bar Restaurants and Restaurant Bars here, I've eaten and or/drank in the majority of them. The ones that I haven't yet, they're listed because I've been recommended to go there by a local or two as they enjoyed them, and they have a great deal. There are happy hours and reverse happy hours listed for many. I enjoyed compiling this, it gave me so many memories, and had me heading to the fridge numerous times what with thinking about food, and so, what do you what what, I hope you enjoy reading it, and that it gives you great ideas for what you could eat and drink. Oh, and to save you plenty of money too! That's obviously da big oi-dee-a (phonetic Dublinese – the big idea).

This list was assembled Spring 2019

NOTE: If you're reading this, and you work in one of the Bars or Restaurants mentioned, and if you believe that I need to update an item or a price, please contact me and I'll happily sort that.

Just before you read the list remember, there are some quite simple ways to save money on food and drink in Las Vegas outside of the deals that you're about to read.

1) Obviously as per this list go to Happy Hours and Reverse Happy Hours (later in the evening from 9 pm, depending on the place, I've listed a good few for you) for food and drinks

2) Find coupons for restaurants and bars. You should be able to get some when getting your players card in the casinos (you can get cards in all casinos) and pick up a Vegas2Go magazine, as they normally have coupons. They're in most food stores, sometimes in cabs, or your concierge should be able to direct you to the magazine.

3) Buffets can be great value. Of course, ideal for those that might only eat once per day. They can lack a bit in flavour at times, I find though. Saying that The Buffet at Wynn is special. You could save money on these buffets by having them included in your hotel deal or if you can't, then perhaps you might go in and pay for a very late breakfast (breakfast price) and you'll be there when the lunch food comes around, or go in (very late) and pay for a lunch and you'll be there when the more expensive dinner buffet comes on. Cheeky? For sure it is!

4) Play the penny slots slowly in the casino and the waitresses will be with you to offer you a free drink. If you intend hanging around there for a while, getting maybe a drink each time, 5 times or so, tip a fiver for

the first one and the waitress will get back to you quite quickly for the second round. I'd give a couple of dollars for each then or a dollar if money was tight. Much MUCH cheaper than you'll pay in the clubs, and you could always do this pre-club if you liked.

5) I'll have many more deals for you here if you want them. I'm hand-picking these.

**The Strip (or very close by, and including the Hard Rock area)**

**Stripburger and Chicken**

(3200 S Las Vegas Blvd) at Fashion Show Mall, opposite Wynn and Palazzo.

These are Happy Hour prices and are available 4 pm-7 pm and 10 pm  to close

$3 – Bud Light, PBR, Coors Light, all on draft

$4 Tap of the day, Sierra Nevada, Pyramid Hefeweizen, Blue Moon, Fat Tire

$4 Well Drinks (Vodka, Gin, Rum, Tequila Blanco, Bourbon, Scotch)

$2.50 Mini Burgers or 3 for $7

$2.75 Mini Cheese Burgers or 3 for $7.75

$5 Loaded Nachos

$-2.75 Hand-Cut Cheddar Fries

$6 Chicken Wings

## El Segundo Sol

(3200 S Las Vegas Blvd) at Fashion Show Mall, opposite Wynn and Palazzo

These are Happy Hour prices and are (4pm to 7pm, in bar area only), opposite the Wynn at Fashion Show Mall

$5 Loaded Nachos (Cheese, Guacamole, Sour Cream, Pico De Gallo)

$6 Quesadillas Chicken, Beef or Cheese) Chicken Simmered with Tomato and Cilantro, Braised Beef or Melted Jack & Manchego Cheeses

$3 Tacos (include Chipotle Steak, Grilled Chicken, Pork Belly, Braised Pork, Rock Shrimp, Braised Beef, Vegetable)

$3 Bud Light Draft

$4 Beer Draft – Pacifico, Modelo, Negra Modelo, Dos XX Lager, Dos XX Amber, Stone IPA, Tap Del Dia.

$4 glass of red or white sangria

$4 well drinks (Vodka, Gin, Rum, Tequila Blanco, Bourbon, Scotch)

$5.50 selected Margaritas (magnificent)

$4 El Jimador Blanco or Reposado Tequila Shot.

$6 Tequila Del Dia Shot

## Sushisamba

(3327 S Las Vegas Blvd) at Grand Canal Shoppes at Palazzo

These prices are for Samba Hour which is Sunday – Friday 4 pm to 7 pm, and 11 pm to close

$5 Crispy Yellowtail Taquitos

$6 Edamame, Shishito Peppers, Wagyu Gyoza, Samba Fries, Eggplant Robata, Organic Chicken Anticuchos, Shrimp Anticuchos, Chili-mint Rock Shrimp Tempura, Whole Squid Robata, Chicharron De Calamar, Crispy Hokkaido Scallop

$8 Wagyu Beef, Sweet Sesame Baby Lamb Chops

$6 Sushi (each) including Yellowtail Tiradito, Salmon Tiradito, Shrimp Ceviche, Spicy Tuna Roll, Ezo Roll, Amazonia, Shrimp Tempura Roll

$7 Cocktails including Caipirinha, Classic Mojito, Lychee Cooler.

$5 Cusquena (Peruvian Malt Lager)

$6 Kirin

$6 Canyon Road Cabernet, Torrontes

$6 Sake "10,000 ways" Eiko Fuji Ban Ryu Honjozo

$7 Prosecco NV Prosecco Piccini

**Tacos El Gordo**

(3049 S Las Vegas Blvd) just heading towards The Strat after Encore

$2 – $2.50 Tacos. These are gorgeous Tacos and super value.

## Blondies Las Vegas

(3663 S Las Vegas Blvd #183) in the Miracle Mile

$20 All you can drink wells and domestic drafts between 3 pm and 6 pm or 10 pm to 1 am

## Ellis Island Pub and Cafe

(4568, 4178 Koval Ln) behind Bally's

$7.99 Top Sirloin Special Filet-Cut. Top Sirloin Steak, served with your choice of potato or rice, garlic green beans and home-made soup or salad. You need to sign up for their players' card in the casino to avail of this and gamble a fiver. Well worth it.

$6.99 for a 10oz Steak and Eggs Breakfast

$2.25 Beers (they brew their own) $2.25 for a draft.

$5 for wings, sliders or a hot dog and fries during the NFL games.

$1 Beers on offer for the Las Vegas Golden Knights Ice Hockey games which is practically every second or third night during the season.

## Stage Door

(4000 Linq Ln) beside Bally's

$2 Coronas

$3 Beer and Hot-dog Special

$1 PBR

## Mon Ami Gabi

(3655 S Las Vegas Blvd) at Paris

These items are on the lunch menu. Mon Ami Gabi, I call it Mon Ami, it should be a part of every trip folks. WOW, so good! Sit out on the patio though.

$14.95 Croque Monsieur (ask for it with mash instead of fries, I'm an Irishman, this is really good mash) and if you have a seat on the patio, you're totally winning.

$15.95 Ham and Cheese Crepe (do the mash trick with this too)

## Bar at Times Square

(3790 S Las Vegas Blvd) at New York New York

These are Happy Hour Prices and they are daily 4pm to 8pm

$5 Bulleit Bourbon Shooters

$6 Ciroc Vodka Cocktails

$6 Don Julio Margaritas

$25 Bud and Bud Light Buckets

## In-N-Out Burger

(3545 S. Las Vegas Blvd) at Linq Promenade, there are multiple locations

$6.70 Double-Double Burger, Hand-cut French Fries and Medium Drink. As fast-food goes, this is very good. Very good quality fast-food.

## Flour & Barley – Brick Oven Pizza

(3545 S Las Vegas Blvd) at Linq Promenade.

These are Happy Hour 2pm – 6pm Monday – Friday and 10pm to close Sunday – Thursday

$5 Draft Beer

$5 Fireball Shots

$6 Well Cocktails

$7 Glass of House Wine

$10 Signature Cocktails

$6 Garlic-Cheese Bread

$8 Chicken Wings

$8 Loaded Pizza Fries

$10 Pizzas including Margherita, Gianna, Bianca, Big Apple, Mushroom.

## Gordon Ramsey Fish n Chips

(3545 S Las Vegas Blvd) at Linq Promenade

$15.98 for Chips and three pieces of fish. Not mega cheap but really tasty. Lovely dipping sauces include Tartar Sauce and Curry & Mango

## Secret Pizza Place

(The Boulevard Tower, 3708 S Las Vegas Blvd Level 3) in Cosmopolitan (Hardly a secret now...)

One of the nicest Pizzas I've had in Las Vegas.

$4.50 Cannoli

$5 Slice of Pizza (very tasty, you'll want two though, two slices of this and the Cannoli and you'll be nicely full)

## Haute Doggery

(3545 S Las Vegas Blvd L-30) at Linq Promenade

$7.99, listen, I know it's a hot dog and it's $7.99 but it's good! A hot-dog called "The Fun-Ghi". char-grilled frank, grilled mushrooms, caramelized onion, gruyere cheese, & truffle mayo. Very lovely! Would I buy it again? Yep!

## Margaritaville Casino's 5 O'Clock Somewhere Bar

(3555 S Las Vegas Blvd) at The Flamingo

5 CENT beers – Miller Lites (that's 5 cents if you needed me to clarify) every day from 5 to 6 p.m.

## Hussong's Mexican Cantina

(3930 S Las Vegas Blvd) The Shoppes at Mandalay Place)

These are Happy Hour Prices – Every Day 3pm-6pm ALSO during ALL Pro-Football and Vegas Golden Knights Games

$3 Select Drafts, Sauza Blue Shot

$4 Well Cocktails

$6 Original Margarita

$15 Bottomless Sangria or Bottomless Mimosas

$3 Tacos

$5 Potato Skins

$5 Tot-Chos

$5 Tostada

$5 Carnitas Sliders

$5 Sopes

## Ocean One Bar & Grille

(3663 Las Vegas Blvd S) Miracle Mile Shops

3-for-1 cocktails all-day

$3 beers all day

$4.99 for a lunch item (includes Grilled Salmon Salad and 1/2 lb. Sirloin Burger amongst other options)

## Emeril's New Orleans Fish House

(3799 S Las Vegas Blvd, Las Vegas) at MGM Grand

These are Happy Hour Prices 2pm to 6 pm and 9:30 p.m. to close.

$5 Bottled Beers (Coors Light, Corona/Corona Light, Budweiser/Bud Light)

$7 House Wine (Red, White, Prosecco)

$7 Well Drinks

$8 Cocktails (Bam Drop, The Classic Margarita, Citrus Mojito)

$9 Chicken and Waffles

$9 Angus Beef Sliders

$10 Braised BBQ Beef Poutine

$10 Grilled Marinated Beef Satay

$11 Vietnamese Shrimp Toast and $12 Smoked Salmon Scotch Egg

**Casino Royale**

(3411 S Las Vegas Blvd)

$2 Michelob bottles. These used to be $1. Still a good deal though! ☺

**RockHouse**

(3377 S Las Vegas Blvd) Grand Canal Shoppes at Venetian/Palazzo

These are Happy Hour Prices (2pm – 7pm) Monday to Friday

$10 Domestic Pitchers

$10 Vodka and Red Bull

$5 Jameson

$5 Patron

**Trevi**

(3500 S Las Vegas Blvd) Located next to the 'Fountain of the Gods' in the heart of The Forum Shops at Caesars Palace.

These are Happy Hour Prices (2pm-6pm and 9pm to close and in Bar Area Only)

$4 Classic Frozen Bellini

$5 Bottle Beer (Bud Light, Budweiser, Coors Light, Corona Extra, Miller Lite, Peroni)

$7 Wines by the glass

$7 Pomegranate Cosmo, House Made Sangria, Rye Lemonade, Strawberry Paradise

$6 Tomato Bruschetta

$6 Stuffed Portobello Mushroom

$6 Fried Calamari

$6 Eggplant (Aubergine) Crisps

$6 Homemade Meatballs

$6 Grilled Meatball Sliders

**Buddy V's Ristorante**

(3327 S Las Vegas Blvd) Grand Canal Shoppes at The Venetian and The Palazzo

Happy Hour is Sunday – Friday (4pm to close)

$1.50 Domestic Beers

$3 House Wines and $3 Sangria

$5 Specialty Cocktails including Passion Fruit Mojito, Basil Fresca, Italian Porto, Sicilian Tea, Rum Punch

$5 Lasagna Nachos, Hoboken Wings, Caprese, Meatball Sliders, Sausage and Peppers, Ravioli Fritto, Salumi and Cheeseboard

$7 Pepperoni Pizza, Margherita Pizza

## Searsucker

(3570 S Las Vegas Blvd) at Caesars Palace

These are Happy Hour Prices (5pm – 7pm daily)

$2 Oyster (each)

$4 Crispy Chicken Sliders

$3 Bone Marrow (each)

$5 Stella

$5 Seasonal Local Brew

$6 House wine (Red, White, Sparkling)

$9 Specialty Cocktails including Margarita, Snake in the Grass, Manhattan.

## Gordon Ramsay Pub and Grill

(3570 S Las Vegas Blvd) at Caesars Palace

These are Happy Hour Deals and they are 2pm – 5pm Monday to Friday and in Bar and Pub area

50% off all draft beer and all wine bottles

$6 Glass House Wine

Under $5 Hellfire Wings, Pigs in a Blanket, Mini Pub Burgers, Warm Salty Pretzels, Truffle Fries

**Bahama Breeze**

(375 Hughes Center Drive) This is slightly East of the Strip.

Happy Hour Prices Monday – Friday 4pm – 6pm, Sunday -Thursday 9pm to close

$3.25 14 Oz Draft Beers

$4.25 20 Oz Draft Beers and Bottled Beers

$4 Classic Cocktails

$5 Specialty Drinks (Mojito Cubano, Ultimate Pina Colada, Classic Margarita, Pineapple-Coconut Martini, Frozen Bahamarita)

$2 OFF Wines by the glass (6 Oz)

50% off Appetizers Including (Beef Empanadas, Firecracker Shrimp, Chicken Quesadilla, Lobster & Shrimp Quesadilla, Skillet-Simmered Jerk Shrimp, Coconut Shrimp, Lump Crab Stack, Spinach Dip &

Chips, Jamaican Chicken Wings, Tostones with Chicken, Buttermilk Chicken Jibaritos, Calamari)

## Ferraro's Italian Restaurant and Wine Bar

(4480 Paradise Rd) close to Hard Rock

These are Happy Hour Prices and only available with the purchase of a drink (tap water not included) – 4-7 PM In the bar, lounge and patio only. Not valid with any promotions.

$6 Rapini, Polpette, Arancini,

$8 Cesare (Caesar Salad) Gnudi, Calamari Fritti, Caprese

$10 Pizza Salsiccia, Uovo Fritto, Cozze in Guazzetto, Costone Calabrese

$12 Peperone Ripieno, Spaghetti Polpette, Pizza Capricciosa, Il Bergese

## Beerhaus

(3784 S Las Vegas Blvd) at Park MGM

Happy Hour Prices Here 2pm – 6pm

$4 Hot Dogs

$4 Select Draft Beers

$5 City Dog (Spicy Mustard, Kraut, Relish)

$5 Loaded Tater Tots (Cheese, Bacon, Sour Cream)

$5 Deviled Eggs

$5 Hand-Cut Fries and Beer Cheese

$5 Fresh Chips and Onion Dip

## DogHaus Biergarten

(4480 Paradise Rd #800) close to Hard Rock

Happy Hour Prices here also and they are Monday-Friday 3pm-6pm, Monday-Thursday 10pm-close and Sunday 3pm-close

$1.49 Tots or Fries

$2 off Draft Beer and Wine

$2 off Well Drinks

$2.99 Sliced Sausage

$3 PBR 16oz Can

$3.99 This Burger

$3.99 That Burger

## Pub365

(255 E Flamingo Rd) at Tuscany

Happy Hour deals here. 3pm – 6pm and 11pm – 2am daily.

$1 off all draft beers and $2 off all small bites

$5 House Wine

$5 Well Drinks

## Maggiano's

(3200 S Las Vegas Blvd) at Fashion Show Mall opposite Wynn. (Italian)

These are Happy Hour prices and it's Monday through Friday 3pm – 6pm

$3 Draft Beers

$4 Flatbreads

$5 Select Wines by the Glass

$6 Specialty Cocktails

**House of Blues**

(3950 S Las Vegas Blvd) in the Shoppes at Mandalay Place (Southern Dishes)

These here are Happy Hour deals and they are daily between 2pm and 5pm and in the bar only.

$6 Jalapeno Cornbread, Mac and Cheese, Garlic Chicken Fries

$8 Chicken Tenders with French Fries, Flatbread (Margherita, BBQ Chicken or Foothills), Popcorn Shrimp with remoulade

$12 Gator Bites (with Nashville Hot Sauce and Ranch), Slider Sampler (Pulled Pork, Angus Beef, Brisket CAB, 1 of each) Brisket Nachos CAB

$6 Well Cocktails, Fireball Shot or Sauza Blue Tequila Shot, Select Beers

$7 House of Blues Private Label Wine, Call Cocktails, Sangria.

$8 Blues Mobile Cocktail, Moscow Mule, House Margarita

## 107 SkyLounge

(2000 S Las Vegas Blvd) at The Strat (HIGH up in the sky in The Strat) (Modern Food)

Incredible View, Delicious food, I think that this could be a great spot to bring a partner or a possible partner.

These are happy hour prices also and are 4pm – 7pm

50% off cocktails and appetizers

## AmeriCAN – beer and cocktails

(3545 S Las Vegas Blvd) at Linq Promenade

$5 beers 2pm to 7pm

$5 Miller Lite Drafts

$5 Jägermeister Shots

$7 Guinness, Guinness Blonde and Black and Golds

$20 Miller Lite Buckets

## Yard House

(3545 S Las Vegas Blvd) Linq Promenade but in Multiple Locations. Really good spot. I'd never refuse food at Yard House.

These are Happy Hour prices, Monday – Friday 3pm to 6pm and Sunday – Wednesday 10pm to close.

1/2 Price Poke Nachos, Ahi Sashimi, Pork Lumpia, Spinach Cheese Dip, Queso Dip, Chicken Nachos, Chicken Lettuce Wraps, Fried Chicken Tenders, Classic Sliders, Onion Ring Tower, Wisconsin Fried Cheese Curds, Fried Calamari, Moo Shu Egg Rolls, Pork Lumpia, Boneless Buffalo Wings, Boneless Firecracker Wings, Boneless Ancho BBQ Wings, Boneless Korean Wings, Gardein™ Wings, Fried Mac + Cheese, Pepperoni & Mushroom, Pizza, Cheese Pizza, Margherita Pizza, BBQ Chicken Pizza, The Carnivore Pizza

$2 OFF All draft beer, wine, spirits and cocktails.

$3 OFF 9 Oz Wine

$4 OFF Half Yards

## Foundation Room

(3950 S Las Vegas Blvd) Mandalay Bay

These are the Happy Hour prices and it's called "Nibbles and Sips" Sunday – Thursday 5pm – 8pm.

Please note: For complimentary admission RSVP at FDRLVReservations@livenation.com with the subject RSVP: Nibbles and Sips.

$5 New Amsterdam Vodka Cocktails

$5 House Red and White Wine (Seekers)

$10 Market Cauliflower Tempurs

$10 Chicken Tikka Skewers

$12 Skirt Steak Skewers

$12 Korean Fried Chicken and Bao Buns

## Rao's at Caesars Palace

(3570 S Las Vegas Blvd)

Happy Hour Prices Sunday through Thursday 5pm – 7pm at Bar Only

$4-$5 Beers

$8-$9 Wine by the glass

$8-$15 Food Specials

## YOLÖS

(3667 S Las Vegas Blvd) Planet Hollywood (Mexican Grill)

The following are Happy Hour and Lunch Specials. Lunch is Monday through Friday 11:30am to 3pm and the Happy Hour is Monday through Thursday 3pm to 6pm in the bar only.

$10.95 Lunch Specials include Street Tacos, YOLÖS Burrito, Tostada Salad. Add a Margarita for $6

## Stripsteak

(3950 S Las Vegas Blvd) at Mandalay Bay.

Happy Hour prices are 4pm through 6pm

$4 Select Beers

$8 Specialty Cocktails

$9 Well Drinks and Select Wines

## El Nopal Mexican Grill

(2000 S Las Vegas Blvd) at The Strat, they have other places at Russell Rd, Decatur Blvd and Craig Rd but these prices are for The Strat

Happy Hour 4pm to 7pm every day and these are Happy Hour prices

2 x 1 Micheladas

$2 Beer

$5 Nachos (any meat)

$5 Breakfast Burrito (Breakfast Hours)

## Twin Peaks

(3717 S Las Vegas Blvd #285) Planet Hollywood area

FREE Rock Wall Climb (all day every day)

$6 Margaritas (all day every day)

$6 Captain and Coke (Monday)

$7 Miller Lt, Coors LT (both 22 Oz) (Monday)

$5 Rolling Rock 22 Oz (Tuesday)

$6 Good Wine (Wednesday)

$7 Dirty Blonde, Knotty Brunette 22 Oz (Wednesday)

$7 Budweiser, Bud Light, both 22 Oz (Thursday)

$7 Proper No. Twelve, Jack Daniels, Crown Royal (Friday)

$6 Bloody Marys, Mimosas (Saturday and Sunday)

$20 Buckets 5 Domestic Beers (Saturday and Sunday)

$25 Buckets 5 Import Beers (Saturday and Sunday)

$12.99 Domestic and $13.99 Crafts in 32 Oz Vegas Size Souvenir Mugs (take them to go) on Saturdays and Sundays

Happy Hour here is weekdays 3pm-6pm

$4 10 oz girl size drafts

$6 22 oz man size drafts

$5 wells

1/2 off all appetizers excluding Wings, Nachos, Hunter's Board and Sampler.

## Cabo Wabo Cantina

(3663 S Las Vegas Blvd, Entrance at the North Miracle Mile Shops)

These are Happy Hour prices and are Monday through Friday 3pm to 7pm

$6 House Drinks

$12 for 2 Sammy's Beach Bar Rum drinks

$3.50 Domestic Draft Beer or $12 Pitcher

$4.50 Import Draft Beer or $16 Pitcher

$24 Bucket of Corona

$6 for 3 Tacos (Chicken, Carnita or Vegetable)

$3 for 2 Taquitos

$5 for 2 Chimichangas

$6 for 3 Sliders

## Double Down Saloon

(4640 Paradise Rd) Close to Hard Rock

Birthplace of the Bacon Martini and home of the famous Ass Juice.

Happy Hour every day 12pm through 5pm and these are Happy Hour prices

$2 Beer

$2 Cocktails

$2 Shots including their famous "Ass Juice"

## Culinary Dropout

(4455 Paradise Rd) at the Hard Rock Hotel and Casino

These are Happy Hour Prices and they are Monday through Friday 3pm – 6pm but not available on concert nights

$5 Well Cocktails and Draught Pints

$6 Sangria

$7 Double Blind, Oyster Shooter, Airplane Pickleback

$3 Hand Cut French Fries

$4 House Potato Chips and Onion Dip

$6 Today's Chopped Salad

$6 Smoked Salmon Bruschetta

$7 Meatloaf Sandwich

$8 Antipasti

$8 Pretzels and Fondue

$8 Shrimp and Chicken on a Stick

$9 Pork Belly Nachos

**Fogo De Chao – Southern Brazil Cuisine**

(360 E. Flamingo Road) East Las Vegas

Happy Hour is Monday – Friday and it's 4:30pm – 6:30pm and these are the Happy Hour prices

$4 Brazilian Bites & Beers

$6 South American Wines

$8 Brazilian Inspired Cocktails.

## Lawry's The Prime Rib

(4043 Howard Hughes Pkwy) Opposite Tuscany Suites heading East

Happy Hour is Monday through Friday from 4pm to 6pm and the deals are

1/2 price on Select Beverages

1/2 price on Select Bar Bites

## Morton's Steakhouse

(400 East Flamingo Road) Opposite Silver Sevens, East Las Vegas

Happy Hour is Sunday through Thursday 5pm – 6pm and the Reverse Happy Hour is Sunday through Friday 9pm – 11pm and these are the Happy Hour prices for both at the bar

$5.50 Select Beer

$7.50 Wine by the Glass

$8.50 Mortini's and Cocktails and $7-$8 Bar Bites Menu

## P.F. Changs

(4165 S Paradise Road) Beside Silver Sevens, East Las Vegas

Happy Hour is 3pm – 6pm and these are the Happy Hour prices

$5 Cecilia's Dumplings – Chicken or Vegetarian (4), Hand-Folded Crab Wontons (4), House-Made Egg Rolls – Pork or Chicken (2) Vegetable Spring Rolls (4)

$6 Chang's Lettuce Wraps (Chicken or Vegetarian), Cauliflower Tempura, Crispy Green Beans, Spicy Tuna Roll, California Roll, Tempura Calamari & Vegetables

$6 Blushing Geisha, Twisted Whiskey Sour, Honey Thyme G&T, Asian Pear Mojito, Red Sangria, Moscow Mule, Organic Agave Margarita

$6 Wine includes Pinot Grigio, Esperto Chardonnay, Kendall-Jackson Garnacha Blend, Los Dos Cabernet Blend, Colby Red

$6 Gekkeikan Sake

$4 Beer – any craft

## Pink Taco

(4455 Paradise Rd) Hard Rock Hotel and Casino, East Las Vegas

Happy Hour here is Monday to Friday and it's 4pm to 6pm BUT excludes concerts nights in The Joint. These are the Happy Hour prices

2 for 1 Beer

$7 Well drinks, wine and Mi Casa Margaritas

$7 Half Order Zonkey Nachos, Honey Chipotle Wings, Grilled Octopus, Vampiro Tacos, 6" Sonroan Street Dog, Jalapeno Relleno Tacos, Chicken Taquitos

## Satay Thai Bistro & Bar

(3900 Paradise Rd, Suite N) East of the Strip

Happy Hour is Monday to Friday and it's 4pm to 7pm and these are Happy Hour Prices

$4 Singha Beer

$30 Singha Beer Tower (equivalent to 8 bottles of beer)

$4 Coors Light, Sangrias, House Wines

$4 Martini's & Tropicals

## The Barrymore

(99 Convention Center Drive) Just beyond Encore on the way to The Strat, close to Peppermill

These are the Social Hour Prices and they are valid Monday through Saturday 5pm – 7pm

$2 Beer Budweiser, PBR (Pabst Blue Ribbon), Bud Light, Rolling Rock

$5 Well Cocktails

$5 Glass Red or White Wine, bottle is $20

$6 Rose Glass or $25 for the bottle

$5 Kir (Creme De Cassis & White Wine)

$5 Red Sangria Glass

$4 Beef Slider

$4 Hand-cut French Fries

$7 Iceberg Wedge

$7 Barrymore Caesar

$8 Smoked Bacon

$8 Roast Bone Marrow

**Benihana**

(3200 Las Vegas Blvd S Suite 1250) At Fashion Show opposite Palazzo

These are Happy Hour prices from Monday – Saturday 12 – 6pm. Available in the Sushi Bar, Lounge and Patio for dine-in only and not available with any other promotion.

$4.50 Pick from Edamame, Seaweed Salad, Salmon Nigiri (2 pieces) or Tuna Nigiri (2 pieces)

$5.50 Pick from Philadelphia Roll, Vegetable Tempura, Pan-Fried Beef Gyoza Dumplings

$7 Shrimp Tempura and $7.50 Pick from California Roll, Chili Shrimp Roll, Spicy Tuna Roll, Fiery Shrimp Tempura, Shrimp Crunchy Roll, Chicken Tempura, Las Vegas Roll

$9 Pick from Poke Appetizer (Tuna and Salmon), Crispy Spicy Tuna, Diablo Wings, Shishito Peppers, Teriyaki Wings

$11 Pick from Dragon Roll, Rainbow Roll.

$5 Hot large Sake and $7 Sapporo large, Seasonal Draft, Kirin Light (12 oz) Lagunitas IPA

$7 Svedka Vodka, Jim Beam Bourbon, Bacardi Superior Rum, Aviation American Gin, Sauza Blue 100% Agave Tequila and $7 Benihana Plum Wine

$8 Nino Franco Prosecco, Gascon Malbec, Coppola Pinot Grigio, Joel Gott Sauvignon Blanc, 14 Hands Merlot, Louis Martini Cabernet, Kendall Jackson Chardonnay

$8 Benihana Punch, Sake Sangria (White Peach, Red Plum), Benihana Mojito (Classic, Exotic, Coconut), Beni-tini, Lychee Blossom, Yuzu Margarita, Whiskey Smash

NOTE: Register for The Chef's Table and receive the latest Benihana news, special offers and a complimentary $30 Birthday Certificate during the month of your birthday. https://www.benihana.com/promotions/chefs-table/

**Bird Bar**

(3555 Las Vegas Blvd South) at Flamingo

There's a Happy Hour from 5pm – 6pm and also additional specials from 6pm – 7pm and also a reverse Happy Hour from 2 – 10am.

50 cent beers at the 5pm – 6pm happy hour! NICE PRICE!

## Cafe Americano

(3570 Las Vegas Blvd S) Caesars Palace

These are the prices for all day every Tuesday

$3 Tacos each (Blackened Mahi, Baja Chicken, Chipotle Shrimp, Short Rib)

$5 Tequila Shot (El Jimador or Silver)

$5 Bottled Beer (Corona, Modelo Especial)

$8 Tequila Cocktails (Palace Paloma, Jalapeno Margarita, Sangria Al Dia)

## Crush

(3799 Las Vegas Blvd S) MGM Grand

Happy Hour here is Monday through Thursday 5:30pm – 7:30pm and 10pm to close

$5 Wines

$5 Draft Beers

$10 Flatbreads including the Artichoke Flatbread with Jalapenos and Caramelized Onions.

## Harvest

(3600 S Las Vegas Blvd) Bellagio

Harvest Hour is 5pm – 6pm and 9pm – 10pm Sunday through Thursday. Harvest wheels around its signature snack wagon during happy hour.

$7 Harvest Signature Cocktails

$7 Wine Selections

$7 Snack Wagon Pop-Up Selections

## Bardot Brasserie

(3730 S Las Vegas Blvd) at Aria

Happy Hour is every day from 5pm to 7pm

$5 Beers

$7 Bartenders Choice Cocktails

$8 Selection of Wines

## Michael Mina Pub 1842

(3799 Las Vegas Blvd S) MGM Grand

These are Happy Hour Prices (all are at the bar) Happy Hours are Monday through Thursday 2pm – 5pm and 9pm through 10pm (Food is for the earlier Happy Hour. Other Happy Hours are Thursday through Saturday 2pm – 5pm and 9pm – 10pm, again food prices are for the earlier Happy Hour on these dates.

$5 12oz Draft

$7 Cocktails, Shot or Wine

$6-$9 Small Plates (includes Pub Tots, Brisket Sliders, Mini Pulled Pork Tacos, Korean Pork Ribs, The Little Wedge, Pail of Fries)

## Mr Chow

(3570 Las Vegas Blvd S) Caesars Palace

Happy Hour here is 5pm – 7pm in the bar and patio lounge overlooking the Garden of the Gods Pool Oasis

1/2 off all drinks

$5 Petite Chicken Sate

$6 Shrimp Rolls

$7 Prawn Toast

$8 Mini Ribs and $8 Minced Beef Pancake

$9 Glazed Prawns

**O'Shea's Pub**

(Linq 3535 S Las Vegas Blvd) Linq

The Happy Hours are Monday through Friday 2am – 6am and 10am – 2pm

$3 Jello Shots, Miller Lite or Coors

$5 Shots

**Once**

(3327 Las Vegas Blvd S) On the second level of the Grand Canal Shoppes inside of the Palazzo. Peruvian Nikkei dining experience

Happy Hour prices again here, Monday – Thursday 5pm – 6pm and Friday through Sunday 3pm – 6pm. These offers are available at the Bar, Ceviche Counter and Patio only and can't be combined with any other discounts or promotional offers.

$5 Draft Beer

$7 Select Wines by the Glass

$8 Well Drinks

$11 Signature Cocktails

$6 Anticucho De Corazon

$6 Anticucho De Pollo

$7 Braised Fennel

$8 Albacore Sashimi

$8 Yuquitas

$9 Tiradito De Corvina

On Friday, Saturday and Sunday from 11am-3pm there are these offers

Bottomless Mimosa (11ma – 2pm) for $25 per person

$6 Two Eggs any style (Egg Whites extra $1)

$3 Bacon

$3 Quinoa Toast

$4 Sliced Avocado

$6 Hand-Cut Fries

## Pampas Brazilian Grille

(3663 Las Vegas Blvd S) Planet Hollywood

These offers are for the Rodizio Brunch 8:30am – 11:30am

$9.95 Rodizio Brunch (over 17 Breakfast and Lunch Items to choose from, including four different types of meat).

$15 All you can drink, 1-hour, Bloody Mary and Mimosa Bar (unlimited add ons +$4)

Brunches do not include coffee, soft drinks or juice and can't be combined with other deals, discounts or offers.

## Phil's Italian Steak House

(3300 Las Vegas Blvd S) TI Treasure Island

These here are Happy Hour prices and it's from 4pm – 6pm

$5 Draft Beer

$8 Wine by the Glass

$8 Mixed Cocktails

$8 Signature Cocktails (Tropical Breeze, The Mule, Sicilian Sour, Desert Sun Tea, Top Shelf Margarita, Empress 1908)

$8 Bruschetta (choose from Lamb, Ribeye, Tomato, Mushroom)

$8 Flatbreads (choose from Grilled Chicken, Margarita, Spinach with Prosciutto and Egg, Meatball and Mushroom

## Pour 24

(3790 Las Vegas Blvd S) New York New York

Happy Hour is 3am to 9am and 4pm-8pm

$6 You call it, domestic bottled beers and well cocktails

There's also a Hockey Game Day Special which is

$5 Hop Nuts Brewery Pint during Gold Knights Games and you can add a shot of Jack Daniels Fire for $5

## Sugarcane Raw Bar Grill

(3355 Las Vegas Blvd S) The Venetian

These are Happy Hour prices and they are everyday 4pm through 7pm

$6 Drafts

$6 Select wines by the Glass

$7 Cocktails

$1.50 Oysters (6 minimum)

$6 Jumbo Shrimp Cocktail (2 pieces)

$6 Brussels Sprout

$6 French Fries

$6 each for American Angus Slider

$6 Pig Ear Pad Thai

$7 Bacon Wrapped Dates

$7 Goat Cheese Croquettes

$8 Mini Salmon Poke Bowl

$9 Mini Maine Lobster Roll (each)

## McMullan's Irish Pub

(4650 W. Tropicana in Spring Valley) Opposite Orleans

There are a couple of Happy Hours

3pm – 6pm and 11pm – 2am (bar and restaurant)

1/2 Price Appetizers (full-size portions, except chicken tenders, Nachos Half Size ONLY at 1/2 off, 12 wings only at 1/2 off)

$1 off all 20oz Draught Pints

$1 off all Well Drinks

Graveyard Specials 11pm – 7am

$1 off all 20oz Draught Pints

2 for 1 Liquor Specials with Casino ID

## The Golden Tiki

(3939 Spring Mountain Rd) Spring Mountain (Slightly West of the Strip)

These are Happy Hour Prices (4pm -7pm)

$5.50 Cocktails – Blue Lagoon, Hemingway's Ruin

$6 Cocktails – World Famous Mai Tai, Zombie Cocktail, Scorpion Cocktail

$5 Captain's Balls, Bad Headhunters Vegetable Spring Rolls

$4 Mermaid Lisa's Sriracha French Fries and $6 World Famous Dole Whip Float w/Rum

## Downtown (Fremont and thereabouts)

## Park on Fremont

(506 Fremont St) Downtown (Modern)

There are the Happy Hours Prices, 4pm to 7pm Monday – Friday. This is really worth a visit to eat. I was very impressed with the food and the price.

$3 Well Cocktails

$4 Domestic Draft Beers

$5 Select Crafts on Draft

$7 Fried Pickles

$7 Mac and Cheese Balls

$7 Garbage Fries (Delicious!)

$7 Blistered Shishito Peppers

$7 Avocado Egg Rolls

$7 Chicken or Beef Taco

**Le Thai**

(523 Fremont St) at Downtown

GO HERE, definitely.

$9.95 Lunch Special You get a nice choice of different curries and meals and you get a drink too, Diet Coke, Coke, Sprite, Iced Tea, Lemonade. Great value this. Great Thai food.

$13 Pad Kee Mow (A.k.a Drunken Noodles) – fantastic, well worth getting. This $13 is the all-day price.

## Hennessey's Tavern

(425 Fremont St #110) Downtown (Irish)

Happy Hour Prices Monday – Friday 4pm – 7pm and some other deals

$5 Number of Happy Hour Drinks including Copper Ridge Wines by the glass, La Marca Prosecco Bellinis, Jumbo Coors Light and Jumbo Blue Moon Drafts, House Made Fresh Squeezed Juice, Moscow Mule, Irish Mule, Black Diamond Margarita, Spicy Margarita, Shots of Tullamore Dew Irish Whiskey, El Charro Tequila, Rumhaven Coconut Rum.

$5 Happy Hour Appetizers including Boneless Buffalo Bites, Cajun Seared Ahi, Crispy Shrimp, Shepherds Fries, BBQ Chicken Sliders, Pesto Hummus

$6 Beer or Well Cocktail and a shot ($6 for both) on Mondays from 9pm

FREE Entree – Flip a coin for a chance to win a free Entree (Wednesday 5pm to close "Luck of the Irish".

50% OFF all bottles of wine (also Wednesday)

$12 Burger and a Beer (on Thursdays) – Any burger and any draft beer.

$5 Hand-made Bloody Mary's (every Saturday and Sunday until 5pm)

$20 Bottles of Champagne (Chateau Ste. Michelle) or Prosecco (Martini and Rossi) with Fresh Squeezed Orange Juice (every Saturday and Sunday until 5pm)

## Downtown Cocktail Room

(111 S Las Vegas Blvd) Downtown (Inventive Drinks and Snacks)

Happy Hour Monday to Saturday 4pm to 7pm, closed on Sunday

50% OFF everything!

## HardHat Historic Lounge

(1675 Industrial Rd, Las Vegas) this is a 12-minute walk from The Strat

Happy Hour Specials (4pm to 7pm)

$1 Tacos (Pork, Chicken or Carne Asada)

$2 (starting at $2) Draft Beers

$3 Bottled and Canned Beers from Local Breweries (up to $7)

$3 Some shots and cocktails starting at $3

$4 House Red, House White

$5 Hardhat Sangria

## Commonwealth

(525 Fremont St) Downtown

Happy Hour is 6pm to 9pm Tuesday through Friday

$3 Coors Light, Bud Light, PBR, House Whiskey, Gin, Tequila, Svedka, Bacardi

$5 House Wine or Dos XX Lager

## Bin702

(707 E Fremont Street, #1220) Downtown at Container Park

 Happy Hour is 3pm – 6pm, these are the prices for this happy hour

$5 Local Pints

$6 Well Drinks

$7 Seattle Cider

$7 Wine by the Glass

$20 Wine Bottle Specials

**Grotto Ristorante**

(129 E Fremont St, Las Vegas) in Golden Nugget, Downtown at Fremont) (Neapolitan influenced Italian)

These are Happy Hour prices 2pm – 6pm Monday through Friday and there's a late-night Happy Hour 10:30pm-12pm Sunday through Thursday. This is available at the Bar only.

$4 Grotto's Famous Peach Bellini

$5 Budweiser, Bud Light, Coors Light, Corona Extra, Miller Lite, Peroni, Rolling Rock

$6 Pinot Grigio, Chardonnay, Pinot Noir, Merlot, Cabernet.

$8 Signature Cocktails including Grapes of Wrath, Limoncello Spritz, Tropical Sunrise, Spaghetti Western

$8 Signature Sangrias and $10 Pizza

## Bocho Sushi

(124 S 6th St #150) Downtown

Happy hour is Monday through Friday 3pm – 6pm This is the Happy Hour offer.

30% off Entire Menu

## Cadillac Bar

(129 East Fremont St) Downtown at the Golden Nugget (Mexican)

These are Happy Hour prices and it's Monday to Friday 4pm – 7pm

$4 Bud Light Draft

$5 Craft and Import Draft Beer including Dos Equis Lager, Tenaya Creek, Sin City Amber

$5 Original Margaritas (Rocks, Frozen or Fruit Flavoured)

$5 Well Spirits (Scotch, Gin, Vodka, Bourbon, Rum)

$6 Fetzer Chardonnay, Fetzer Cabernet Sauvignon, Chateau Ste. Michelle Riesling, 14 Hands Merlot

$6.99 Chicken or Pork Quesadillas

$6.99 Cantina Beef Nachos

$6.99 Cantina Chicken Nachos

$7.99 Ahi Tuna Tacos

$5.99 Street Tacos (2 mini tacos, choose crispy or soft corn tortillas) Spicy Beef, Chicken Fajita, Tejas Carnitas

**Evil Pie**

(508 Fremont St) Downtown

Happy Hour is everyday 2pm through 6pm and these are those deals

$3 Draft Beers

$4 Wells

$20 Pitcher and a Pie

$5 Slice and PBR

## Frankie's Tiki Room

(1712 W Charleston Blvd) Close to North Premium Outlets

$10 Specialty Tiki Cocktails 24 hours a day

$25 Specialty Drinks in Souvenir Mug

1/2 price 1st drink when wearing a Hawaiian Shirt on Friday 4pm through 8pm

$4 Aloha Coolers on Friday 4pm through 8pm

## Hogs and Heifers Saloon

(201 N 3rd St) Downtown

Happy Hour is Monday through Friday 12pm to 4pm

$2 off Domestic Draft Beer

## Hop Nuts Brewing

(1120 S Main St #150) Downtown

Happy Hour everyday 4pm through 7pm

$4 Pints

## La Comida

(100 S 6th St) Mexican restaurant with American rock. Downtown

Happy Hour deals here Tuesday through Sunday 3pm – 5pm

$5 Margarita and there are Beer Specials

## Mickie Finnz

(425 Fremont St #120) Downtown

These are Happy Hour is Hawaiian Happy Hour Monday – Friday 4pm – 7pm

$4 Well Liquor

$4 Coors Light Draft

$3 House Wine by the Glass

$5 Bacon Tots

$5 BBQ Pulled Pork Sliders

$5 Vegetable Spring Rolls

$5 Spinach and Artichoke Dip

Monday Mojito Madness is Buy one Get one on Mojito's all day

Tuesday Two Timin' Tuesdays have 2 for 1 Burgers and 2 for 1 Taco Platters (this offer is dine in only)

Saturday and Sunday 11am – 3pm there are $5 Bloody Mary's

**Nacho Daddy**

(113 N 4th St, also at Miracle Mile Shops, Summerlin and Duluth) Downtown

These are Happy Hour prices and the Happy Hour is 3pm to 6pm Monday through Friday

$5 Well Drinks, Mexican Drafts, House Wines

$5 House Margarita, Strawberry Margarita

$5 Food Specials

Tuesday 8 am through 2am deals are

2 for 1 on any Tequila

$5 for 3 Chicken or Pork Street Tacos

$7 for 3 Steak or Shrimp Street Tacos

## Oscar's Beef Booze & Broads

(1 Main St) inside the Plaza Hotel. Downtown.

Happy Hour is Sunday – Thursday 4pm-7pm and the deals are

50% off appetizers, house wine, well liquors and beer

## Pizza Rock

(201 N. 3rd St) Downtown

Happy Hour is Monday – Friday 3pm – 6pm and late-night happy hour 10pm to close every night

$4 All well drinks

$4 PBR 32 Oz

$2 off all draft beers, wines by the glass and specialty cocktails

$4 Italian Fries

$4 Fried Green Beans

$4 Pizza Rock Meatballs

$5 Zucchini Fries

$5 Personal Pizza with 1 topping

$5 Garlic-Garlic Bread

$7 Personal Size Pizzas including Cal Italia, Pesto Paradise, Tony 2 Times

$8 Personal Size Pizzas including Old Smokey, River City Ranch, Picante

## Rachel's Kitchen Downtown

(150 N Las Vegas Blvd) at the Ogden, Downtown

Happy Hour here is Monday through Friday 4pm – 6pm

1/2 off Beer and Wines by the glass

## Siegel's 1941

(600 Fremont St) El Cortez Downtown

50% off their special menu on Wednesday from 6am to 10pm for guests over 50 years old

$7.77 Breakfast supreme sandwich (Egg, Bacon, Canadian Bacon, Jack and Cheddar Cheese in an English Muffin) 11pm to 11am, seven days a week.

$12.95 for a Prime Rib any time of day or night

## Therapy

(518 East Fremont St) Downtown (I really want to put the ? (question mark) after the word Therapy, in honour of the Irish band of course)

Happy Hour Prices are everyday 2:30pm through 6:30pm

$4 House Wine

$5 Wells

20% Off Food Items

## Triple 7 Brew Pub

(200 N. Main Street, Main Street Station Casino) Downtown

$2.50 Pints of Microbrew, House Wine, Well Drinks (Monday through Friday 3pm-6pm)

$3-$7 Appetizers (Monday through Friday 3pm-6pm)

$2.50 Micro Brew Refill, House Wine, Well Drinks (Monday through Friday 11pm – 2am)

$5 16oz Hand Crafted Microbrew (Monday through Friday 11pm – 2am)

$5 10" Five Cheese, or Pepperoni (Monday through Friday 11pm – 2am)

## Vanguard Lounge

(516 Fremont St) Downtown

1/2 Off Well Drinks, House Wine and Beer (Monday through Friday 4pm – 7pm)

$7 Hand-Crafted Cocktails (Monday through Friday 4pm – 7pm)

1/2 Off Well Drinks, House Wine and Beer (Saturday 6pm-7pm)

$7 Hand-Crafted Cocktails (Saturday 6pm-7pm)

## Town Square

## Brio

(6653 Las Vegas Boulevard) Town Square – Yummy Food.

These prices are weekdays and in the bar only.

$4 Crispy Smashed Potatoes

$5 Spicy Shrimp and Eggplant

$5 Margherita Flatbread

$5 Chicken Pesto Flatbread

$5 Tomato Caprese

$5 Calamari

$5 Beef Carpaccio

$6 Crispy Shrimp

**West of the Strip**

**Sammy's Woodfired Pizza Flamingo**

(9516 W. Flamingo Rd) Spring Valley, West of the Strip

Happy Hour is daily 4pm-6pm

Half off Shareables and $2 Off Beer and Wine by the Glass

NOTE: Sign up on their site and receive a FREE pizza on your next visit! New Insider E-Club members will receive a FREE PIZZA with a purchase of equal or greater value. This special offer will be emailed to new members upon confirmation of signing up. Here's a link for them... http://www.sammyspizza.com/vip-club/

## Sagos Baja Tavern and Lounge

(5020 Spring Mountain Road, #7)

Happy Hours are everyday 3pm through 7pm and 11:59pm to 3am

$2 Wells and Domestic Drafts

$4 Craft and Premium

1/2 off Wine

$5 Select Appetizers and Sliders

## Other Mama

(S3655 S. Durango Unit #6) Spring Valley, West of the Strip

Happy Hour is 5pm-6pm daily

$3 Draft Beers (PBR, Firestone Union Jack, Asahi, Tenaya Creek, Modelo Negra, Weinstephan)

$5 House Wines (White, Red or Sparkling)

$5-$7 Kitchen Appetizers

$8-$9 Raw Bar Selections

All Day Every Sunday and Monday $1 Oysters and 1/2 off Wine Bottles

**Multiple Locations**

**Pt's Gold, PT's Brewing Co, Sean Patrick's, Sierra Gold and SG Bar**

Happy Hour is 5pm-7pm and late night 12am-2am

50% off drinks (includes Blue Moon, Stella Artois, Grey Goose, Patron and Woodford Reserve)

$6 Sriracha Chicken Bites or Loaded Potato Skins $7 1/2 lb. Pub Burger or Chicken Parmesan Sliders

$8 Flatbreads: 3 Cheese, Meat Feast, Gilroy or Buffalo Chicken

Food specials are obviously not valid at non-kitchen locations.

## THE END! (Only for now...)

Thanks for reading!

Shane(r).

# CREDITS FOR IMAGES

(All images have been altered)

COVER - https://pixabay.com/photos/las-vegas-game-casino-gambling-82319/

FAQ'S - https://pixabay.com/photos/las-vegas-game-casino-gambling-82319/

ORANGE QUESTION MARK - https://pixabay.com/users/Clker-Free-Vector-Images-373

LAST MINUTE BOOKING - https://bbook.com/news/celebrities-react-las-vegas-terror-attack/

TEACH ME - https://pixabay.com/photos/vegas-casino-gambler-poker-1224246/

FLY - https://www.flickr.com/photos/63122283@N06/20427694494

MON AMI GABI - https://commons.wikimedia.org/wiki/File:2012.10.04.170606_Bistro_Paris_Hotel_Las_Vegas_Nevada.jpg

LE THAI - http://lethaivegas.com/

ELLIS ISLAND VILLAGE PUB AND CAFE -
https://www.ellisislandcasino.com/

EL SEGUNDO SOL http://elsegundosol.com

PEPPERMILL LAS VEGAS -
http://peppermilllasvegas.com/

ISBN: 9781700318121

Printed by Amazon KDP in the United States of America.

Disclaimer: Events in this book are my memories and from my perspective.

First Printing, 2019.

www.shanelovesvegas.com

Printed in Poland
by Amazon Fulfillment
Poland Sp. z o.o., Wrocław